T0010362

Brutish Necessity

A Black Life Forgotten

Brutish Necessity

A Black Life Forgotten

Jon Berry

Winchester, UK
Washington, USA

JOHN HUNT PUBLISHING

First published by Chronos Books, 2021
Chronos Books is an imprint of John Hunt Publishing Ltd., No. 3 East St., Alresford,
Hampshire SO24 9EE, UK
office@jhpbooks.com
www.johnhuntpublishing.com
www.chronosbooks.com

For distributor details and how to order please visit the 'Ordering' section on our website.

Text copyright: Jon Berry 2021

ISBN: 978 1 80341 096 8
978 1 80341 097 5 (ebook)
Library of Congress Control Number: 2021950058

All rights reserved. Except for brief quotations in critical articles or reviews, no part of this
book may be reproduced in any manner without prior written permission from the publishers.

The rights of Jon Berry as author have been asserted in accordance with the Copyright, Designs
and Patents Act 1988.

A CIP catalogue record for this book is available from the British Library.

Design: Matthew Greenfield

UK: Printed and bound by CPI Group (UK) Ltd, Croydon, CR0 4YY
Printed in North America by CPI GPS partners

We operate a distinctive and ethical publishing philosophy in
all areas of our business, from our global network of authors to
production and worldwide distribution.

Contents

For all those who strolled with me, so blissfully unaware of the society unfolding around us, up St Luke's Road, Hope Street, Varna Road, Calthorpe Park and skipping blithely through all that Balsall Heath – not Edgbaston – had to offer.

But most of all, for two men whose lives should be rescued from obscurity. Gentleman Thomas Bates, selling fags and papers and strolling down to the county ground. And poor, bewildered Oswald Grey: a stranger in a cold, unwelcoming land, drifting into petty and fateful crime.

Again brutish necessity wipes its hands
Upon the napkin of a dirty cause

A Far Cry From Africa
Derek Walcott. St Lucian Poet

Foreword by Steven Knight. Film director and creator of *Peaky Blinders*

A big city at the start of the sixties, when the whole world was on the brink of cultural change. A big city actively demolishing its pre-war past and trying to construct a post war future. A city where new arrivals from a broken empire were challenging old certainties.

Birmingham in 1962 was a place of uneasy compromises which, at the same time, was exploding with the vibrancy of new cultures, new music, the tastes and smells of other worlds. Set in this volatile environment, *Brutish Necessity* tells a tragic true story which also shines a light on a whole era and an entire chapter of British history.

Beautifully written by Jon Berry, *Brutish Necessity* does justice to the story of an injustice without scoring points or banging drums. At times, funny and poignant, you feel the pulse of the city as you read, and perhaps begin to understand more about the present by learning from the past.

Some things have changed, some things have stayed the same. *Brutish Necessity* goes some way to explaining how and why.

Preface

This is a book with a terrible event at its centre. The sort of event that no longer happens. It's not a book reliant on lurid, graphic description, but much of what follows will often make the modern reader wince. And occasionally smile. And think – I hope.

It's a book about race, immigration and prejudice. It's about how some attitudes have changed while others remain stubbornly the same. The central, terrible event has a downtrodden victim, but the book is not about victimhood. There's no argument here about the inevitability of discrimination. There are tales of agency, determination and joy. But it's most definitely about swimming against a tide.

It's a book about class, values and attitudes. It's about how the great bodies of the state – parliament, the law, police, press and broadcast media – reflect ideas that look to the past and which rarely threaten to challenge the status quo.

There is mystery and there are shocking tales. Shocking whether they take place in down-at-heel bedsits or shocking when they're in judges' chambers. Some of the central characters have disappeared untraceably; others died well-fed and contented in their beds.

Every fact has been checked, every quotation is real and attributable. All statistics and figures are a matter of public record. This is a book about finding some truth: its own credentials are impeccable. There may be opinion here, but there is no fabrication.

It's a book about the city in which I grew up, blissfully unaware of the physical roughness of my surroundings. The blunt dismissiveness from adults, whose stoic post-war refusal to be easily impressed – or shocked – was just normal behaviour. Like the city I come from, nothing that follows is sentimental.

It's an attempt to save a name from total obscurity.

And so, to the terrible event.

Chapter 1

The evening paper and the return of the blood-stained man.

It begins with a childhood memory that turns out to have been false.

This is what I thought I remembered from a gloomy afternoon in November 1962.

Some context to begin with. I was nine years old and lived in Institute Road, King's Heath in Birmingham. I was the youngest of three children. I lived with my two teenage sisters and my widowed mother. My sisters went to grammar school and college and I, of course, was still at primary school. My mother worked full-time, usually in a minor bookkeeping or accountancy capacity. Like many people of her generation, she had left school at 13 with few official qualifications, but her quickness and certainty with figures ensured she was always employed.

I was always the first one home. I had a key and, once in, I was entrusted to light the coal fire in the living room and to get on with any homework I might have been given. More often than not though, once the fire had taken, I'd go into the back yard and thump a ball against the wall, enjoying an hour or so before any nagging neighbour returned to cluck and moan.

On this particular evening, my mother returned as usual at about 5.30 and, just as usual, was carrying the local paper. And now the memory goes wrong. This is what I thought I remembered.

'Anything good in the paper, mom?' reaching out to grab a look.

And at that point, my mother snatches it away from me.

'Don't go looking in there today. Nothing in there for you.'
And then she says, seemingly out of nowhere, 'A crowd of them

waiting outside. What did they think they were going to do?' I'm used to her returning from work frayed and impatient, but this time her irritation has a different quality.

And, of course, I'm totally foxed.

'Who, mom? Where was there a crowd?' And at this point, my younger sister, in her mid-teens, comes into the kitchen – the natural meeting place, notwithstanding the fire now blazing in the living room.

'Do you mean the hanging?' she asks. 'At Winson Green?'

I know there's a prison in Birmingham and I know it's at Winson Green and the reason I know is that when we're in the playground and someone's been particularly bad, somebody else will pipe up that you'll have to go to Winson Green. But to be honest, it might as well be on the moon. It's actually less than six miles away, so, as I say, to a nine-year-old in Birmingham in 1962 – the moon. But a hanging? What? Outside? Like some of those dreadful history-type things I've read? It might just have been that distorted image, cooked up in a childish imagination – a public execution on the streets where I lived – that accounts for this whole thing lodging so firmly in my consciousness.

'Was it a murderer?' I want to know.

'Yes.'

'Was it the blood-stained man?'

'Oh, you and your blood-stained man.' And now, with some relief, my mother has reverted to the much more familiar and comfortable role (for me) of exasperated, impatient parent.

Some time before this incident – which did take place, notwithstanding my imperfect recollection – I had seen a TV news item about a crime committed in Birmingham from which the alleged perpetrator, a blood-stained man, had escaped on a number 8 bus. Now I knew about the number 8 bus because it was one that I sometimes caught. What's more, the picture accompanying the news item showed a bus seat – and I'd sat on one of those too. So, the blood-stained man had caught the number 8, like I did, and had sat on a seat, like I did. That was as close to real-life horror as I wanted to get. I was an avid reader with an over-active imagination: for a few weeks, I became worried and obsessed by the blood-stained man. I looked with lingering trepidation for any sign of his departed presence on every bus I got on – and I got on plenty. From the reflective distance of almost sixty years, I can empathise completely with my mother's frustration when, thinking he'd evaporated, he made his reappearance on that dank evening. We'll learn a little more about him in Chapter 3.

'But was it him?'

'It doesn't matter who it was. He's dead now and he won't go killing anyone else, will he?'

'That'd be students outside,' offers my sister, for whom, no doubt, the very thought of students with their freedom and bohemianism represented the glamour that her teenage self craved so enthusiastically. 'Protesting against the death penalty.'

This draws some harrumphing from my mother who, in common with most people of her background and life experience, has little time for such fine feeling.

'Is that what's in the paper, then? Can I have a look?' Lunge.

'No. Keep your hands to yourself.' Her shortness sharpened, no doubt, by the prospect of more nightmares and fretful anxiety on my part now that the spectre of the blood-stained man has made an unwanted reappearance.

And so it was that my mother kept the evening paper from me, safeguarding me from the stark headline about an execution in my city, taking place against a background of righteous picketers.

Except that some of it can't be entirely verified.

That I had such a conversation about a man being hanged at Winson Green Prison is something I simply couldn't have made up, not least because the memory of it, however hazy, has haunted me since. That it must be the one that took place in

November 1962 has to be the case because prior to this execution, the last one in Birmingham was in 1958 when I was just five years old. What's more, a murder did take place in Birmingham some five months earlier in June 1962 and the suspect was initially reported to have made his getaway on a number 8 bus – a detail which was to resurface at the trial of the man hanged in November 1962. But there is one crucial part of the story which I am unable to verify.

Memory has convinced me that my mother must have been sheltering me from a distressing headline. No such headline exists – at least in the extensive digital archives now available to us. On 20 November, the day of the execution of Oswald Augustus Grey at Winson Green Prison, four local newspapers in the UK reported it briefly in the evening editions, only one of which, the *Coventry Evening Telegraph*, could be deemed to be remotely local. Its brief coverage, like that of the *Belfast Telegraph,* the *Aberdeen Evening News* and the *Liverpool Echo,* was tucked away in the middle sections of inside pages. In Belfast, the story merited smaller headlines and fewer words than the revelation that the Senate had insisted on controls ensuring that water content in butter remain at no more than 15%. In Liverpool, train delays due to wire theft merited more attention, while in Aberdeen the new look for post offices was deemed more exciting. Maybe my mother was carrying the paper from the day after the hanging – 21 November?

But by then, Grey's execution must, indeed, have been yesterday's news because the only newspaper to report it was local – The *Birmingham Daily Post.* Here is the entire article which was, once again, on an inside page:

Hanged in Birmingham

Oswald Augustus Grey, a Jamaican baker of Cannon Hill Road, Edgbaston, was hanged at Winson Green Prison, Birmingham yesterday for the murder of Mr Thomas Arthur Bates, an Edgbaston newsagent. He was found guilty and sentenced to die at Birmingham Assizes for shooting Mr Bates, aged 47, in his shop in Lee Bank Road, Edgbaston on June 2. Uniformed and plain-clothed police stood on duty outside the prison gates as four students from Birmingham University paraded with anti capital punishment placards. Grey was the first to be hanged at Winson Green since August, 1958 and the youngest since 1949 when a 19 year-old soldier was executed for strangling a 14-year-old girl in Sutton Park.

This book will attempt to unpick the detail embedded in this piece of blandness. It is possible that my mother was carrying an evening paper for which records don't exist in the British Newspaper Archives and that she was, indeed, offering me some protection. There may have been a screaming headline that can no longer be located and which, indeed, did become the next day's fish wrapping. Quite how four students with some placards became a crowd is something we'll never get to the bottom of – nor, indeed, why this detail so irked her. She's not here to ask, so I'll never know.

What is beyond dispute, however, is that the 117 words in a newspaper from the city where a young Black man was executed in 1962 is entirely typical of the scant, dismissive coverage of his alleged crime and eventual punishment. What follows attempts to illuminate an event that has lodged, however imperfectly, in the imagination of that nine-year-old and which still has plenty to tell us about race, justice and social attitudes sixty years on.

Chapter 2

Oswald Grey. Forgotten, unreported and nobody's cause celebre.

The evening of 2 June 1962 in Birmingham was cool for early summer. It was recorded as 57 Fahrenheit, or just below 14 Centigrade. There are some other recorded certainties. First, newsagent Thomas Arthur Bates was shot and killed in his shop in Lee Bank Road at about 6.30 p.m. His death certificate records him as 47 years old, despite press reports that vacillate between 46 and 47. He lived in the house, of which his shop was part, with his mother, Louisa Bates, who was 79. Second, at 7.45 a.m. on 20 November, some 26 weeks after the crime, Oswald Augustus Grey was hanged for his murder. Grey was convicted on 13 October and his appeal was heard 16 days later. Just over three weeks after that, the execution was carried out at Winson Green Prison by hangman Harry Allen.

To modern sensibilities, this dispensation of justice all seems rather rushed, but despite my own alarm on first reading about this, it turns out that such official haste was entirely normal. A law of 1834 had softened the harsh edict of 1752 that allowed for a mere two days between sentence and execution, by stipulating that at least two Sundays had to pass between the two events. By 1863, this had been extended to three Sundays and this was the law that was in place until the abolition of capital punishment in Great Britain in 1965. Only six more victims went to the gallows in the UK after Grey's death.

This rush to punishment is in stark contrast to what we now know when it comes to those countries still enforcing this drastic penalty. The only two major industrialised democracies which still execute people are Japan and the USA and in both cases, time spent waiting for the act to be carried out can be extraordinary.

In the case of the former, the average time for those who are eventually executed is seven years; in the USA it is 13. In the bizarre case of Thomas Knight, who was executed in Florida in January 2014, he had been on Death Row for 39 years.

Another, more gruesome – and gruelling – contrast exists. Executions in the United States in recent years have been bedevilled by botched and elongated processes. This has often, but not exclusively, been the case when so-called lethal injections have been used. Redolent of the images of kindly vets soothing loved pets toward their dreamy end, such events have sometimes been more like unwatchable clips from horror films. The notorious case of Joseph Wood in Arizona in 2014 is among the most disturbing. Injected over 15 times with extraordinary doses of midazolam and hydromorphone, Wood took over two hours to die. The sturdy yeoman that is the British hangman would have shaken his head in dismay at such inefficiency.

The execution of people in modern Britain is inextricably linked to the name of Pierrepoint. Not just one Pierrepoint, but three: this was a family enterprise. The bulk of Britain's post-war hangings were conducted by Albert Pierrepoint, who continued the occupation of his father and uncle, Henry and Thomas respectively. They had all been busy. Thomas had presided as principal officer on 261 occasions, Henry on 75 and Albert was in charge 169 times. His tally had been enhanced by his deployment at home and abroad in hanging war criminals and he proudly claimed that he had despatched William Joyce, the German propagandist and one of the last two people to be hanged for treason, in eight seconds. This sharp efficiency, nurtured as part of the Pierrepoint tradition, was a hallmark of the professional pride that such men – or so their memoirs would have us believe – brought to the job.

Oswald Grey's final moments were entrusted to Harry Allen. He had acted as assistant to Pierrepoint on several occasions and with Grey's demise had officiated in some capacity in 80 executions. He performed his duties on two further occasions after 20 November 1962. On one of these in December 1963, Robert Douglas was a young prison officer delegated to be present for the final few hours of Russell Pascoe at Bristol Prison, who was to be hanged by Allen. His account, given to the *Guardian* newspaper in 2014, talks of Allen as brash, almost boastful, when in the company of officers and colleagues the night before the execution – although he makes full allowance for some excusable, public bravado. More sombrely, he talks of how Allen comes to the condemned cell to talk to Pascoe, who he reassures and to whom he is courteous and respectful. When he leaves, the terrifying realisation dawns on Pascoe that Allen had, literally, been sizing him up.

Somehow, Robert Douglas performs his duty of keeping the prisoner calm until, at about a minute to eight in the morning, Allen enters the cell, leaves an unfinished cigarette in the ash tray, looks Pascoe in the eye and tells him to 'do exactly as I say, son, and it will all be very quick and easy'. Douglas doesn't see Pascoe again. He is led from the room as the clock strikes eight and moments later, he is dead. From being taken from the cell to the trap doors opening, fourteen seconds have elapsed. Allen returns and takes a draw on his cigarette. He responds to Douglas's enquiry as to whether Pascoe was any bother by telling him that he was 'as good as gold'.

In 2008, Stewart McLaughlin, a serving prison officer at Wandsworth at the time, penned Harry Allen's biography. The trim paperback offers a broad-brush insight into parts of Allen's life and the final chapter uses some of the subject's own words to illuminate these. The bulk of the book, however, concerns itself with the crimes and potted versions of the trials of those executed by him. None of these offers the unsettling detail that characterises Douglas's account of his last hours with Pascoe. McLaughlin's account of Oswald Grey's alleged crime and its investigation is, as later pages here will reveal, just a touch slipshod, written, as it was, for the more lurid end of the true crime market. The entire episode is dealt with in fewer than six short pages and there are no revelations concerning Allen's conduct or subsequent commentary.

The paths of Allen and Robert Douglas had already crossed before Pascoe's execution at Bristol. When Allen carried out his duty in Winson Green Prison in November 1962, Douglas was serving there. His own memoirs dedicate a few pages to Grey's internment and demise, even though he, or his editor, persist in misspelling his surname throughout his folksy account. Douglas talks of the way in which the very presence of a condemned man permeates the atmosphere of the entire prison and of how, every time he passes Grey's cell in the line of his normal duties, he is conscious of the fact 'that just the other side of that wall sits a man who is under sentence of death'.

What then follows, in Douglas's account of the days leading to the execution, jars the sensibilities of the modern reader. His book, *At Her Majesty's Pleasure*, was published in 2007. It is neither sensationalist nor self-aggrandising; in fact, its charm lies in the way in which the writer has illuminated anecdotes and episodes with lively reported dialogue along with entertaining insights and reflections. Unlike many commentators who look back on their language and actions, Douglas has offered no disclaimers or apologies for using terminology that was commonplace at the time. It may be an unfair assumption, but one might have hoped that by 2007, he could have taken note of this and admitted to a degree of embarrassment about some of his reportage.

Looking back from 2007, he has no problem with his generic labelling of the Black prisoners in Winson Green as West Indian and of seeing them, as do his colleagues, as Grey's 'fellow countrymen'. What's more, Douglas tells us, 'West Indians are VERY superstitious folk' (his emphases) and so when he plays a little trick on one of them four days before the hanging – 'I can't resist it – the Devil makes me do it' – he has to 'bite the inside of my lip so as not to laugh'.

The jape goes as follows. Bernard, a 'good-natured West Indian kid' approaches Douglas. 'Boss, can I axt you sum'ting?' His question is this: the rumour among the Black prisoners is that the nearer Oswald Grey's day comes, 'he done turning pale!' Is it true, Bernard needs to know? Before the Devil gets hold of Douglas, he reassures him that it is not, before leaning in to him to tell him that, actually, he'd already 'gone nearly as white as me'. Bernard's 'pupils roll almost out of sight'. Poor soul that he is, he shouts, 'T'anks, boss' then 'shoots off along the landing and vanishes into a cell where three black guys are ... he obviously wants to be the first to confirm it's true'.

Douglas forbears to inform us of the hilarity that no doubt ensued in the staff canteen on his re-telling of this comical deception. There would be no surprise whatsoever if both the language and outlook behind it were entirely accurate, reflective as they were of common attitudes to Birmingham's first wave of immigrants from the Caribbean. What remains unsettling, and telling, is that from a distance of some 45 years, the narrator of this tale seems blithely unaware of how offensive his account now sounds. This all-pervasive, oblivious racism, as we shall see as this story unfolds, lies like a shroud over the case of Oswald Grey and the times in which he lived and died.

Whether or not it was Grey who shot and killed Thomas Bates on that June evening in Birmingham, one thing is certain. The brevity with which his case is dealt with in the biography of the man who hanged him is indicative of how the case remains almost entirely unknown. His conviction and execution have excited almost no interest since they occurred. Six months earlier, James Hanratty was hanged at Bedford by Allen, by then firmly established as the senior practitioner of the trade. The thirty pages McLaughlin dedicates to this episode demonstrates the stark comparison between what we know about the two cases. There are obvious reasons why.

Hanratty had been convicted of the murder of Michael Gregston and for the attempted murder and rape of Valerie Storie. The offences took place on 22 August 1961 in a layby on the A6 near the Bedfordshire village of Clophill. Gregston, married but separated, had been parked up in his car in Dorney Reach, Buckinghamshire, with Storie, a workmate from a laboratory in Slough. It was there that they were accosted by a man, unknown to either of them, carrying a gun. After a prolonged evening of threat, uncertainty and a good deal of directionless driving around, the culprit shot Gregson and then raped Storie before shooting her and leaving her for dead. She survived, severely paralysed and became the chief witness for the prosecution.

Hanratty was not arrested until the following January, largely because of a convoluted set of investigations that reflected his life of petty crime and periodic stints of incarceration. This all furnished him with a platoon of people providing detectives with conflicting stories, all made ever more difficult to disentangle because of withdrawn and unreliable testimony. This intricate web of evidence is brilliantly dissected in *Who Killed Hanratty?* written in 1971 by the late investigative journalist, Paul Foot. It is because of the tenacity of Foot, along with a range of other journalists, campaigners and public figures, that Hanratty's case retains a place in the public consciousness, whereas Oswald Grey, with no such champions, remains almost totally forgotten.

Reflecting the alacrity with which punishments were carried out, Hanratty was found guilty on 12 February 1961, his case went to unsuccessful appeal on 13 March and he was hanged on 4 April – the three-Sunday rule being strictly observed. If the authorities thought the case would evaporate into history, they could not have been more mistaken. Contemporary newspaper reports of his demise were marginally more detailed than those of Grey, but not to any great extent. The *Birmingham Daily Post* afforded Hanratty three times as many words as they later did for one of its own citizens, but this didn't amount to much of a splash in terms of column inches. Nevertheless, the resolve of the campaigners – the most high-profile of whom was John Lennon – ensured that it would be another forty years before there was even a hint of closure on the case. Convinced that there had been a miscarriage of justice and that this was further proof of the precarious and unreliable nature of capital punishment, they had the money, connections and resources which have been instrumental in making the murder of an amorous scientist on a rural backroad one of the most recognisable of modern times.

Their efforts helped to bring about the first exhumation of Hanratty's body from Bedford Prison in 1966 to be taken for burial near his aunt in Watford. There followed three separate Home Office enquiries in 1967, 1975 and 1996 none of which impacted on the original conviction. As advances were made in the use of DNA, Hanratty's body was exhumed once more in 2001. Samples from his corpse matched both mucus on the handkerchief in which the murder weapon had been found under the back seat of a number 36A bus, as well as semen on the underwear of Valerie Storie. All the same, in 2002, the Court of Appeal expressed its certainty about the 'overwhelming proof of the safety of the conviction from an evidential perspective'. The appellants, led by the eminent human rights barrister, Michael Mansfield, maintained that the DNA samples could easily have been contaminated, but to no avail. Some forty years after his execution, the book on the death of James Hanratty was closed, albeit possibly only temporarily.

His trial had lasted for 21 days, a record at the time. The breadth of the investigation meant that details about his family, life and background became widely known. In common with many who were executed in the post-war years, his was a life characterised by a lack of educational achievement followed by involvement in disorganised, chaotic petty crime. All of this was compounded, as is so often the case, with a series of physical accidents and mishaps. The trial revealed him to be part of an underworld that was more Laurel and Hardy than Kray and Richardson. Nevertheless, lurid tales of raunchy trysts in laybys, double exhumations, the miracle of extracting DNA from long dried snot and sperm, along with a small army of wealthy do-gooders convinced of his innocence, meant that the case of James Hanratty remains a perennial favourite of the world of 'true crime' publications – even though it all appeared to be the bungled and clumsy work of a confused, disappointed and probably vulnerable young man. He was 26 years old when he died.

'We are moving in a rather strange world,' said the prosecutor. 'We are among people who steal guns, who traffic in guns, people who live aimless lives in night clubs and dives.'

These were, indeed, the words of a prosecutor – just not about the world of James Hanratty. Applicable as they may have been to him, Mr Graham Swanwick QC, prosecuting for the Crown, was reported to have used them to describe the circumstances of Oswald Grey in Birmingham some six months later. Grey's trial lasted a mere five days. Because nobody took up his cause, we know only that he was described as a 'Jamaican baker'. As we will see, his world appeared to be just as loose and dysfunctional, it's just that the perfunctory nature of his trial and the investigations that preceded it allows us nothing like the insight into that of Hanratty.

Hanratty's was not the only *cause celebre* in terms of its appeal to those fighting for the abolition of the death penalty. In March 1950, Timothy Evans was hanged at Pentonville Prison for the murder of his wife and daughter: Albert Pierrepoint conducted the execution. He was present again at Wandsworth in January 1953 to oversee the demise of Derek Bentley and back at Pentonville in July of the same year to ensure some kind of rough justice as John Christie met his end for the crimes of which Evans had been falsely accused. Two years later he was on duty again, this time at Holloway Prison, to hang Ruth Ellis, the last woman in Britain to suffer such a fate. All three cases were soaked with ample spicy material to enflame the imagination of film and documentary makers, enabling them to construct passionate and lurid tales, all close enough to the known facts of the crimes to be both convincing and to ride on the right side of legislation and defamation. The most cursory of internet searches prompts page after page of information of varied quality and credibility about these cases. The lives of Evans, Bentley, Christie and Ellis can be pieced together with a degree of accuracy. The same is not true of Oswald Augustus Grey. Unemployed Jamaican baker, Oswald Grey. The evidence for whose conviction, flaky as some of it was, has never excited anything like the same attention.

There are some minor, irritating inaccuracies in Stewart McLaughlin's account of the environment in which Grey was supposed to have murdered Thomas Bates in June 1962, none of which detract from a story written for impact rather than close analysis. However, in his summary of the situation faced by Grey, his judgement rings as true – truer, in fact – in 2021 as it did when he made it sixteen years earlier:

Was Grey as guilty as he superficially sounds? This was Britain in the 1960s, remember, when the first wave of immigrants was settling down in a climate of some hostility. The British way of life, and of doing things, was new and foreign to them. Oswald Grey might have been bewildered by the events following his arrest. He would have been the only Black man in the police station, possibly the only Black man on remand; white lawyers and white policemen would have surrounded him. He would have been in an alien world.

There were 211 executions in the UK once the Second World War concluded in May 1945. Of these, less than a handful were Black men: Grey, Mahmood Hussein Mattan – whose story we will hear in a moment – and Backarey Manneh, who was hanged in 1952 and who will resurface in Chapter 7. There had been other executions of Black men on British soil prior to the end of the war. On 8 May 1945, Victory in Europe Day, Private

George E Smith from Pittsburg was hanged at Shepton Mallet Prison for the murder of a diplomat, Sir Eric Tiechman, who had accosted Smith and a friend whom he suspected of poaching on his land in Norfolk. The gaol at Shepton Mallet was used to house US military prisoners and between 1942-1945, eighteen of them were executed. Thirteen of these events bore the stamp of a Pierrepoint, usually Thomas assisted by Albert. In statistics that ring true decades later, ten of the 18 were Black and three Hispanic. In terms of the legalised killing of civilians, once the war ended, there were cases involving men who had emigrated from eastern Europe and some prisoners of war, five of whom were executed on the same day in October 1945 for beating and stringing up one of their own officers in a camp in Corrie, Perthshire. For the main part, however, the perpetrators of some 200 capital crimes were very much home born and bred.

History has dealt very differently with the cases of Mahmood Hussein Mattan and Oswald Grey. Mattan was convicted for the murder of shop owner, Lily Volpert, in Cardiff in March 1952 and was hanged for his alleged crime six months later. Born in what was then British Somaliland, he worked as a merchant seaman, fetched up in Wales in the late 1940s and married a local woman with whom he had three children. The couple separated in 1950 but continued to live in different dwellings on the same street. Mattan left the merchant navy in 1949 and at the time of the murder of Lily Volpert was working at the local steel foundry. The evidence against him was disordered, confused and contradictory and any reading of the accounts of the trial suggest that the idea that his conviction was beyond reasonable doubt is risible. But nothing, perhaps, was as outrageously damning as the remark in the summing up of his own defence barrister, T E Rhys-Roberts, that Mattan was a 'half child of nature; a semi-civilised savage'. Quite what was in Roberts' mind by referring to his client in this way defies the modern imagination. If he was looking for sympathy from the jury, he

15

had backed the wrong horse and Mattan, by all later accounts a hard-working citizen dogged by racial abuse and prejudice, was sent for his grim appointment with Albert Pierrepoint and became the last man to be hanged in Wales.

There is a reason why we know a good deal about Mahmood Hussein Mattan. Two years after his death, another Somali, Taher Gass, was convicted of murdering a local wages clerk. There remains widespread suspicion that, what with all these people looking the same, mistaken identity could have been at play in Mattan's conviction. Fifteen years on, the main prosecution witness at his trial, Harold Cover, was found to have attempted murder on his daughter using the same method – a razor – as that used on Lily Volpert. The case against Mattan looked more insecure with the passing of time and these subsequent revelations. But his was not a case that vaporised into obscurity.

He had left a wife and three children, and they worked tirelessly to clear his name. In 1998, Lord Justice Rose declared that the evidence against Mattan was 'demonstrably flawed' and awarded the family £725,000 in damages. The internet search for Mattan's case sparks over a dozen pages; Oswald Grey doesn't quite run to two. In September 2020, a vigil was held in Mattan's memory as part of local Black Lives Matter campaigning. However appalling the circumstances of this dreadful miscarriage of justice, he has made a stamp on history.

Whereas Oswald Augustus Grey, unlike Hanratty, Evans, Christie, Bentley and Ellis, merited just 117 words in his local newspaper and appears lost to popular memory. What follows tries to explain why.

Chapter 3

Saturday evening, 2 June 1962. The fatal consequence of no cricket and no pub.

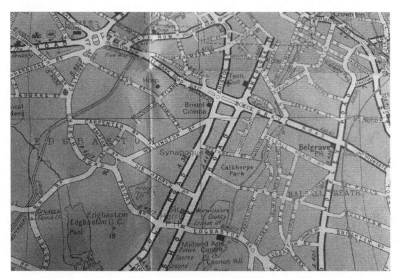

Birmingham 1962

Bartholomew's street map of Birmingham from 1970 shows the Lee Bank area of the city before the construction of the urban highways that now cut their way through it. Lee Bank Road, the location of Thomas Bates's shop, lies north-west of Balsall Heath, the suburb in which most locals would place it, although officially it is located in Edgbaston. Prison officer Stewart McLaughlin's account of Thomas's murder in Harry Allen's biography concurs with this – although, characteristically, he carelessly misspells the road's name. Edgbaston covers a huge area, parts of which are, indeed, quite plush. But McLaughlin's assertion that the road was in a leafy suburb, far removed from inner-city decay, would have most natives spluttering in disbelief. His assertion that it lies 'just round the corner' from the county cricket ground

17

on the Pershore Road, endows the area with bucolic cosiness that bears little reality to the situation on the ground. A keen-eyed reader would be entitled to ask why I seem to be so authoritative about this part of the city, living, as I did, three miles away in King's Heath.

The explanation that follows is not self-indulgence. It attempts to paint a picture of the city as it was at the time, viewed through the eyes of a nine-year-old, but, just as crucially when it comes to imagining the life of Oswald Augustus Grey, through the experience of an immigrant family.

My maternal grandmother and her husband came to England in 1905 from the small town of Szczebrzeszyn, now in Eastern Poland. Even by Polish standards, the name defeats the most stout-hearted: the best approximation is Shrebyeshin. Despite its size, remote location and general anonymity, the town is known by Polish people as part of a tongue-twister of the 'she sells seashells' variety. I discovered this when I first went there and have since delighted a succession of Polish acquaintances with the knowledge, prompting many of them to rattle off the rhyme with varying degrees of success. When my grandparents left the town, which now sits almost directly on the border between Poland and the Ukraine, it was part of Russia; it had been disputed territory for centuries. Fearing the pogroms that were sweeping that part of the world, they made their move. Had they remained and eked out some kind of existence, they would certainly have met their fate some forty years later when the Nazis arrived and forced Jews in Szczebrzeszyn to dig their own graves before shooting them when they had done so.

It's almost certain that when they left their homeland, they were under the impression, like so many who did so, that they were heading for America. The story of how they contrived to end up in Birmingham has been lost in myth, mystery and, literally, translation. Nevertheless, they managed to set up home in Yew Tree Road, unmarked on Bartholomew's map but located just to the west of Ryland Road, south of Lee Bank Road and clearly designated on contemporary maps. They had six children: a son and five daughters. Young men aplenty must have come calling. One of them, in the early 1940s, was my father. He'd been on something of a journey himself.

Until 1938 he had been getting on with a normal, quiet life in Vienna. The street on which he was living, still standing and looking relatively unchanged, is a short walk from the Prater Fairground, where the big wheel became famous for its use in *The Third Man*. A stroll down the row of unassuming, grey apartment buildings, now inhabited largely by people of Turkish origin, might reveal nothing until one looks at the inscriptions on the entrance halls of all of them. There, a list of names appears along with the stark admission that, on various dates in 1938, these people were taken from their homes and, as the blunt translation reveals, murdered by the Nazis. My personal researches reveal that my father escaped this fate by a matter of days, quite possibly hours.

Once again, the detail of quite how he found his way to Yew Tree Road are hazy and do not form a major part of this particular narrative. Nonetheless, it is clear that his journey was dangerous and traumatic and, as is so often the case when people undergo such ordeals, he appeared to have divulged very little about it. His history died with him in 1957 at the unconscionable age of 48 and although my maternal grandmother lived on until 1964, outliving her émigré husband by 28 years, very little of their lives and background was known to me as I drifted my way through my early, naturally self-obsessed years. What endures is often informed more by understandably romantic interpretation than hard fact.

What is indisputable, however, is that in common with many immigrant communities, my family sought out those who shared common experiences and chose to live in the same area. For Jewish immigrants in Birmingham in the first decades of the century, the part of the city they looked to was the area around Lee Bank Road. Having settled there, they established, in time-honoured fashion, their shops, places of worship and education. Bartholomew's map shows the Central Synagogue located in its current position on the Pershore Road (Birmingham people will always use the definite article when describing this thoroughfare). It had moved there from its location from a former Methodist Hall on the Bristol Road, just south of Wrentham Street, in 1961. The map does not show the location of the city's other principal synagogue, Singers Hill – the one favoured by my family – located on Blucher Street, just north of Holloway Head. Neither, unsurprisingly, does it mark the Birmingham Hebrew School in St Luke's Road, just west of Lee Bank Road off Belgrave Road. These, though, were the major landmarks in my life.

In common with most immigrant communities once established in their new homeland, my extended family moved on to more genteel and comfortable surroundings. Following the usual patterns of migration, different groups moved in to take the places they had vacated. In Birmingham from the late 1940s, those people often originated from the Caribbean. My recollections of how my relatives spoke of such people and the language they used to do so still make me shudder, even though I now acknowledge that there was little going on that hadn't happened for centuries. They were, of course, expressing relief that it was no longer they who were at the bottom of the pile. However, even from nearly sixty years away, the fact that that they saw nothing contradictory in expressing such views strikes me as peculiar. For it all, the usual pattern of migrant behaviour was established. As they moved out, the darkies moved in.

My mother and father may have moved out to King's Heath, but that had no effect on my native's knowledge of the Lee Bank area. Despite there being a perfectly good primary school yards away on Institute Road, my parents insisted on their children attending the Hebrew School on St Luke's Road, a fifteen-minute ride on the 48 bus through Moseley and into Balsall Heath. They also insisted on something else. On two days a week and on Sunday mornings, we were to receive more specific religious education provided by the Central Synagogue. This was called cheder, from the Hebrew for 'room' but used more commonly in Yiddish for an elementary school. Strap yourself in for a journey into the past of central Birmingham in the early 1960s.

When school finished, those of us who had to go to cheder – about a dozen or so – would walk, unaccompanied, to the Central Synagogue. Prior to 1961, this was located on the Bristol Road. There were various ways through the back streets that we could employ, our first challenge being to avoid the kids from Hope Street School who hated yids. The highlight of the journey, however, was the diversion via the slaughterhouse in Wrentham Street. If we were lucky, we'd see the pigs being unceremoniously channelled to their unhappy demise: other days we'd just hear a variety of disconcerting grindings and screeching from within. What we'd also see was poverty, dirt and deprivation on a scale that is now almost unimaginable. As is the way of childhood, this constituted nothing other than the familiar backdrop to our lives. And then there were the bum buildings – or at least that's what I thought they were called. These were the bomb-sites – swathes of rubble, rusted steel and assorted debris – as yet unaddressed since the Luftwaffe had done its work. Bombed, not bum, buildings: the best open playgrounds little boys and girls could ever have wished for.

From 1962, cheder moved to its new home on the Pershore Road, so the quickest and easiest way to get there was to nip straight down Varna Road. It's not called Varna Road now. So notorious had it become as the hub of the city's red-light district in the 1960s, attracting national red-top attention, that when it was eventually knocked down and redeveloped, the city's authorities chose to consign the name to history and dub it Belgravia Close. As the *Daily Mirror* pointed out in a daring, publicly spirited investigation into vice girls in 1969, 'what the Street Offences Act could not do, a bulldozer did'. All the same, at no point in the early 1960s, did anyone think it fit, or necessary, to advise a small group of primary school children not to walk down it. For a startling and illuminating set of images – poverty, prostitution, immigration, bombed buildings – Janet Mendelsohn's collection, entitled simply *Varna Road*, is a window into a world that we may have lost but which was utterly familiar to my nine-year-old self and, almost certainly, to Oswald Augustus Grey. And whoever gave Stewart McLaughlin the impression that it was a 'world away' from inner-city deprivation had grievously misled him.

The county cricket ground – another major landmark of my younger days, as it happens – was not, as the *Mirror's* vice investigation suggested 'a six hit' from the area, but a good mile or so down the road. Thomas Bates was a frequent visitor and his elder brother, John, who lived nearby in Sun Street, expressed surprise that he had not gone to watch the cricket on the day of his murder. He told the *Birmingham Daily Post* that he 'used to go and help my brother out in the shop practically every weekend. He was very keen on cricket and I expected him to go and watch the first Test (an international match) at Edgbaston on Saturday, but he decided not to go, and we watched some of it on television instead.'

Perhaps Thomas had decided that the day's play held out little promise of excitement. England's cricketers were playing Pakistan, a team relatively new to international cricket. The game at Edgbaston was only the eighth meeting between the two teams and although Pakistan had recorded a famous victory in 1954, it would be another twenty years and thirty matches until they did so again. Thomas would not have needed to purchase a ticket in advance in the days when turning up and paying at the door was the norm. Neither could he have imagined that a similar fixture played some forty years later would attract a huge local audience, the majority of whom would be rooting for their heroes from the distant, native land of their heritage. He may simply have looked at the close of play score on Friday evening, saw the visiting team some 400 runs behind with five wickets down and predicted, quite rightly as it turned out, that Saturday's play would be a very one-sided affair.

Besides, a good deal of the game was on TV on the BBC and so John and Thomas Bates were able to see some of the action from the comfort of the house behind the shop itself. Maybe Thomas had stayed behind to mind the shop so that his partially blind 79-year-old mother, Louisa, who helped out in the shop, could enjoy the televised spectacle of the Trooping of the Colour in the morning – broadcast in full, in black and white. John Bates left Lee Bank Road that evening at about 6.30, just as play was ending at the cricket and shortly before his brother, on hearing the shop bell, left the sitting room and encountered his assailant.

John's usual practice was to mind the shop while Thomas took his mother for an early evening drink, but on 2 June 1962, they decided not to go out. They would not be making their appearance at the Welcome Inn as usual. Could it have been the lure of the appearance on ITV's *Thank Your Lucky Stars* of crooner Matt Munro or sparkly pianist, Winfred Atwell? The show was recorded live, just the other side of the city centre at ATV's Aston studio. A favourite moment was always when local girl, Janice Nicholls, would pronounce her seal of approval on a new record release by informing us that she would 'give it foive'. Or maybe Louisa and her companion, 76-year-old Sally Hodgkinson, were waiting for the cricket to end so that they could enjoy risqué comic Terry Thomas or glamorous singer Helen Shapiro on *Juke Box Jury* at 6.30. *The Ken Dodd Show* and *Perry Mason* were on afterwards; not a bad night's telly.

Whatever the reason, Thomas Bates was neither making his way back from the county ground nor setting off to the pub. He responded to the bell clanging in the shop and went to sell cigarettes, sweets or, possibly, that evening's *Sports Argus*, the local Saturday night pink sports' newspaper, full, no doubt, of England's dominance at Edgbaston and Warwickshire's promising (but ultimately futile) first day against Kent in Folkestone. We now approach the limit of what is indisputable. Louisa Banks heard a noise from the shop and went into it to find Thomas lying on the floor. An ambulance was called, but he died on his way to Birmingham's General Hospital in Steelhouse Lane, a matter of moments away.

According to the *Birmingham Post*, Louisa had heard a 'shot' and went, with her companion into the shop. There they found the place in disarray and Thomas lying on the floor. However, she initially suspected that Thomas, who had endured poor health since his stomach operation eight months previously, had suffered a heart attack. It later transpired that the bullet that killed him had gone straight through his heart, lungs and liver, lodging in the wall behind him, so drawing such a conclusion was entirely reasonable. Thus it was only as events unfolded that it became clear that her son had died from a gunshot wound.

Poor John Bates was distraught about the unfortunate timing of his departure that evening. Perhaps he shouldn't have been quite so surprised at what happened. The shop was the second of its sort belonging to the Bates family. The first, located a little further north on Lee Bank Road had been demolished as part of the early post-war redevelopment in the area six years previously. Since its relocation, it had been raided twice, albeit not during business hours, with cash and tobacco stolen. The last occasion was less than a year before the events of 2 June. The area was one where petty crime frequently occurred, but John would probably not have considered armed robbery to have been likely when he left that evening. He confirmed to the *Post* how unusual it was for his brother not to have taken his mother to the pub on a Saturday evening. 'Normally I would have been there. I wish I had been.'

As it happens, he was back at his post in no time at all. He was there next morning sorting out the Sunday papers on the wall outside the shop, aided by his two sons, as detectives around them searched for clues. The policeman in charge was Detective Chief Superintendent Gerald Baumber and we'll return to his efforts in just a moment after a brief pause to explain that, in the most tangential of ways, he has already played a part in the story so far as part of my hazy recall of the day of Grey's hanging. Back in late 1959, Baumber had not yet achieved the rank of Chief Superintendent but was learning his trade as a central part of the team set up to solve one of the city's most notorious, and gruesome murders.

It had taken place just off Lee Bank Road in Wheeleys Road – and my grandmother lived there. Unlike her children who had now scattered to Moseley and King's Heath, she had chosen to remain in the part of the city with which she had become familiar. Now a widow of some twenty years, she must have decided, in modern parlance, to downsize, but limited her horizons to a move round the corner from Yew Tree Road. Her new home was located on the same street as the YWCA – a respectable hostel for single women – and it was there, on 23 December 1959 that the grisly murder of 29-year-old typist Sidney Stephanie Baird by Patrick Joseph Byrne took place. In what must have been a ferocious attack, Byrne sexually assaulted his victim before beheading her. Baumber's superior, James Haughton then did something unique and extraordinary: he used television to appeal for information. His new-fangled ways reaped dividends.

Within hours someone volunteered information – and that someone was a bus conductor on a number 8 bus (I'd caught a number 8 bus) and he told of a man with heavily blood-stained hands who took a seat upstairs, getting off in Small Heath. The blood-stained man on the number 8 bus! Somehow, I must have imbibed the detail of this story and, at six years old, it is no surprise that it gave me the recurrent nightmares that my mother had been so keen to bury.

Haughton's methods put in train a series of events that eventually led to the arrest and conviction of Patrick Byrne, who admitted to the murder and several other assaults. He pleaded guilty on the grounds of diminished responsibility and was sentenced to life imprisonment. What he didn't admit to was being the blood-stained man on the number 8 bus. Heaven only knows, that man may still be at large but has, thank goodness, long since disappeared from my nocturnal consciousness. George Baumber probably learnt a thing or two about looking to the public during the investigation that led to his capture and was not slow to use the power of publicity, this time through the printed media, in an attempt to locate the murderer of Thomas Bates just round the corner from Wheeleys Road in Lee Bank.

His team interviewed family members on the Sunday morning. By then, the local ballistics expert, Mr C W G Hill of the Firearms' Department had located the spent bullet and case in the shop. Their principal witness at the time was a ten-year-old girl, Ann Bradley, who lived in nearby Owen Street – since demolished – who said she had seen 'a man in dark clothing' outside the shop at around 6.30. To give greater weight to this gem of evidence, *The Birmingham Post* of 4 June – the first press coverage of the murder which had occurred too late for the Sundays – decided to print her picture. Whether or not George Baumber approved of something that seems so outlandish to modern sensibilities is not known; what is more certain is that his fascination with the number 8 bus, like mine, was enduring.

During Sunday, he delegated officers to board the number 8 and ask passengers whether they had witnessed anything the previous evening. 'It may be,' he suggested, 'that someone saw something unusual as they passed on the bus at about that time. If so, we hope they will come forward.' Why not, he must have told himself, use a tried and trusted formula? Especially given that, before the next working week had ended, Baumber and his team were pretty convinced they had got their man – or boy.

And that, as far as we know, is what occurred on the early evening on Saturday 2 June 1962 and the hours that followed in the rough-and-ready corner of Edgbaston that abuts the centre of Birmingham. A local newsagent, blandly described in ensuing press reports as 'friendly' was shot in his shop when he might otherwise have been at the cricket or the pub. Six months later a young Black man, 19 at the time of the murder, was hanged for the crime. What sort of life had Oswald Grey led? How had he experienced the city that had become his new home? And, above all, did he kill Thomas Bates and was he afforded justice and a fair trial?

Chapter 4

Hard graft and grey weather; blues parties and church.

To be clear from the start, I'm a white man telling the story of a long-deceased Black man from a distance of sixty years. Although we lived on the same streets – and caught the same buses – there would have been few other points of genuine correspondence between the lives we lived. In my primary school just off Lee Bank Road, the first children of immigrant families were now lightly scattered around the classrooms and, as I described earlier, the streets and houses vacated by immigrant families similar to my own were being passed on to people from the Caribbean and, later, from Britain's former colonies in south Asia. I don't presume, however, to suggest that this furnishes me with anything other than the flimsiest of insights. For much of what follows in this chapter, therefore, I am indebted to the writing, scholarship, testimony and artistic endeavours of those acknowledged here and at the end of this book.

On 1 July 1962, with Oswald Grey remanded in custody and charged with the murder of Thomas Bates, the Commonwealth Immigrants Act came into force. Its passing through parliament marked a clear sea-change in the attitude of the government of the day towards immigration. This was still far from being the toxic topic it would become six years later, fomented by Enoch Powell in his infamous 'Rivers of Blood' speech in Birmingham, but for some Conservative backbenchers – their party had been in power since 1951 and would remain in office until 1964 – it was becoming increasingly important.

In 1948, advertisements had begun to appear in daily newspapers in Jamaica and Trinidad alerting people there to the possibilities of work and opportunity in the 'mother country' –

the centre of the British Commonwealth. Labelled as 'Passenger Opportunities' by the shipping companies, crossings did not come cheap. *The Empire Windrush*, by far the most famous of the vessels coming from the Caribbean, and the one which has given its name to the first cohorts of emigrants from the islands, charged £48 for cabin class and £28 for the troop deck. The most reliable allowances for price comparison suggest that the higher of these prices translates to about £1,100 in modern terms. A quirk of the early adverts was that the timing of departures was approximate, with sailings scheduled to depart, for example, 'about 23rd May' – the first Windrush sailing departed, in fact, on the 24th. Crossings took some 30 days, punctuated for many with inevitable bouts of seasickness, compounded, no doubt, by the nervous anxiety of being uprooted from all that was familiar and the taking of steps into the unknown.

Plentiful job vacancies, particularly in semi-skilled and unskilled occupations, meant that the Labour government of the day was looking to its colonies to address these gaps in the national workforce. Thereafter, a steady flow of immigrants took the opportunity to seek security of employment and a better life for their families. Work was usually easy to find, particularly in labouring jobs in urban areas and the public sector offered reasonable wages in hospitals, the post office and public transport. By the mid-1950s, an estimated 18,000 Jamaicans had come to Britain.

Despite their official invitation, they received a wary reception, sometimes from those from whom better should have been expected. In a shameful period in its history, there is no avoiding the fact that the British trade union movement often went out of its way to obstruct successful integration in parts of the workforce. In the BBC documentary *Has Britain a Colour Bar*, made in 1955, the well-meaning voice over is soaked in unconscious racism, informing us that 'Birmingham people have become accustomed to these dark-skinned strangers' and, in the case of Indian and Pakistani market traders, 'their fiercely competitive ways'. The West Indian, we are told, probably has to start off taking an unskilled work, but this still pays him '£7 a week, much more than he'd get at home, even if he could find a job'.

However, it is in its coverage of West Indian workers on the buses in Birmingham that the film takes a shocking turn. The item starts off cheerily enough with the narrator quoting a local citizen praising how 'they didn't half make a difference on the buses these coloured chaps, wreathed in smiles, even at seven in the morning'. And yet the management at the Hockley depot refuses entry to the film crew fearing, according to the voice-over, that 'we had come to glorify the coloured busmen'. Undeterred, they gain access and speak to district secretary of Transport and General Workers (TGWU), Harry Green, who complains that his members are concerned about the 300 coloured workers who have 'been inflicted' on them and of how 'these people don't mix'. It was an accusation that I frequently heard repeated as an iron truth at gatherings of my own family of immigrant stock – no great mixers themselves.

Following the first wave of post-war immigration, numbers peaked at just under 47,000 in 1956 before falling for three consecutive years. Having dropped to 29,000 in 1959, they increased to 61,000 in 1960 and 141,000 in 1961. Home Office statistics at the time did not distinguish between those coming from Commonwealth countries and the significant numbers coming from Ireland. However, in terms of mainstream political discourse, immigration had simply not been an issue. It had not appeared in any party's manifesto in either of the General Elections of 1955 or 1959. Which is not to deny that for some MPs, numbering fewer than a handful, it was a topic that was gnawing away at them.

Perhaps the most alarmingly colourful of these was Cyril Osborne, the Conservative member for Louth in Lincolnshire.

Quite how many immigrants had made their way to his part of the world by the late 1950s is uncertain, but one would imagine that any black faces there at that time were, as now, something of a rarity. Nevertheless, this did not prevent him from expressing the view, protected by parliamentary privilege and therefore not requiring any evidential proof, that rising immigration was linked to increased levels of leprosy. Osborne also expressed the fear that the conversion of a church in Smethwick into a Sikh temple was a sign that Britain's status as a Christian country was now under threat.

He had few supporters in the parliamentary chamber, but one was Norman Pannell, representing Liverpool, Kirkdale, who was particularly irritated by the amount the British taxpayer was forking out for provision for those children of immigrants who had ended up in care. By 1959, the odd couple that was Osborn and Pannell had found another chum.

Harold Gurden was elected to serve the people of Selly Oak, the neighbouring constituency to Edgbaston, in 1959. A trawl through his contribution to the democratic process during his 15 years in office reveals a record of service so slight that one can imagine that he must have almost literally been laughing all the way to the bank when he picked up his MP's salary. He was one of the founding members of the Monday Club, a right-wing pressure group whose opinions on a range of social topics from 'repatriation' to support for minority, white rule in South Africa, has been a source of both entertainment and wonder since its inception. However, as the tide of opinion about immigration began to shift at the start of the decade following his election, he may have felt that he was, for the moment, on the right side of history.

By 1961, with the number of immigrants having more than doubled from the previous year's 60,000, the House was becoming less relaxed about the issue. Then, as now, much of that disquiet centred on housing and, in an age-old trope that still shouts at us from right-wing quarters, the simplistic correspondence between such shortages and increased numbers of immigrants reared its ugly head. Then, as now, the state had failed miserably in its duty to find enough affordable, comfortable housing for huge swathes of its people. It then compounded this failure by remaining tight-lipped and cowardly while discourses of blame towards immigrants bubbled poisonously along.

In Birmingham, even without the significant amount of damage inflicted by Nazi bombing, the immediate post-war housing situation was dire. In 1947, notwithstanding some early redevelopment to the north of Lee Bank Road and elsewhere, there remained 35,000 dwellings that had to share lavatories. Of these, 6,500 had no separate water supply and 417 still had no access to gas or electricity. In 1957, Prime Minister Harold Macmillan blithely informed the good Tory burghers at Bedford's Conservative Club that 'most of our people have never had it so good'. Yet given the pressing need for decent housing in Birmingham and throughout the country, the council there was still only building dwellings at the rate of 2,000 a year. There had been 50,000 applicants for housing in the city in 1947; this had risen to 70,000 by 1958.

Birmingham Council adopted policies of patching up substandard properties as a stopgap measure while it worked on a wider building plan. Various areas were designated as 'short life' or 'intermediate life' and repairs at correspondent levels were allocated to them. Many residents scornfully referred to this as 'soling and heeling' and the policy led to a situation where those in houses undergoing this remedial treatment lived in the dirt and disruption of uneven building development going on around them.

One such area was Hingeston Street, a couple of miles north of Lee Bank Road and just a mile or so from Winson Green Prison where Oswald Grey met his end. The street was used as one of the locations for director Ken Loach's TV drama, *Cathy*

Come Home. It was filmed in 1966 and broadcast as part of the BBC's *Wednesday Play* series. Dealing with the tribulations of a young couple seeking accommodation for themselves and their baby, it charts their descent into homelessness and poverty in harrowingly realistic detail. It attracted a viewing audience of 12 million people, nearly a quarter of the population, and served to expose a national scandal in a way that seems unimaginable in the modern multi-channelled world where a TV programme viewed simultaneously by a mass audience is almost unknown.

Loach's play captured a housing crisis occurring in 1966 that had its roots stretching back to a time before the war, but which uneven post-war spending had failed to resolve. Little wonder, then, that the political class was feeling edgy about immigration and its association with housing shortages. Minutes of the Home Office Affairs committee in 1961 reveal an increasing nervousness. 'Some members,' it reported, 'were doubtful whether control arrangements based on labour would be effective in conditions of full employment'. In other words, it would be difficult to keep people out when there were jobs to be done, especially considering that this was the rationale for the 1948 British Nationality Act which had prompted Windrush and all that followed. Parliament was also acutely aware of what any restrictive legislation could then look like, particularly if it made the distinction between Commonwealth citizens and those from other parts of the world, including Ireland. The Home Office record speaks for itself:

A number of members were strongly of the opinion that we should think very carefully before embarking upon legislation, on the grounds that to do so would be regarded as discrimination on the grounds of colour. There was, however, a strong body of opinion within the Committee to the effect that legislation would be the only effective means of dealing with this matter.

If the protagonists of *Cathy Come Home*, a young, white couple with a baby, were unable to find accommodation, any Jamaican immigrants watching their semi-fictionalised tribulations would have been nodding on sympathetically. There is some dispute as to the authenticity of the infamous 'No Irish, No Coloureds, No Dogs' sign in a Notting Hill bed and breakfast establishment but that is hardly the point. There is ample evidence in the BBC film archive of signs reading 'No coloureds' or 'No West Indians' as well as others reading 'No Irish, No Coloureds'. Such prejudice was prevalent and unremarkable. It may be that the artefact that has imprinted itself on the national consciousness is something of a confection, but it still captures the unseemly spirit of the age that played out all too practically for many migrants to Britain's towns and cities.

Unsurprisingly, early arrivals from the Caribbean excited great interest. Extensive newsreel footage which, tellingly, focuses almost exclusively on young men – despite there being significant numbers of women who had made the journey – shows them arriving on these shores smartly dressed in suits and dashing hats. Their smiles are nervous, but there is no hiding their obvious excitement at the prospect of the new life before them. Pathe News, bringing the first moving images into cinemas of those arriving on Windrush in 1948, talks amiably of '400 happy Jamaicans' who have come to 'do any kind of job to help the motherland along the road to prosperity'. Happily informing us that 'they're full of hope for the future', the chummy voiceover extols us to 'make them very welcome here'.

Footage from an item later that year presents interviews with some of the immigrants themselves – again, all male. Some are ex-servicemen whose intention is to resume their posts in the UK, but for most, the principal ambition is to acquire any kind of job with decent pay. An interesting thread to the overall commentary, and one that will resurface in these pages, is the notion that for many who have made the journey, their intended

34

stay is only temporary. Lest the 1940s viewer should feel denied of any exoticism tinged with stereotype, Lord Kitchener – the King of Calypso – is approached and happily provides us with two *a cappella* verses of *London is the Place for Me*. The tone of the coverage is overwhelmingly positive and humane.

One could be forgiven for thinking, therefore, that the same agency's output seven years later in 1955 and entitled *Our Jamaican Problem* might be an indication that this early optimism had soured a little. That would not be the complete picture. The five-minute item repays some scrutiny. Once again, smart young men – and, this time, a few women – disembark from their blowy vessel while the voiceover tells of the '10,000 West Indians' who arrived in the UK in 1954 and the 15,000 who are anticipated in 1955. They are, we are reminded in schoolmasterly tones, British citizens and, as such, as entitled to entry as anyone. Post-war Britain, we are informed, is, after all, home to 15,000 of our 'former enemies'. The film then cuts to a gloomy-looking street in Lambeth and runs us through a few eminently respectable households who have made their life in this lesser Eldorado. Those who are parents, we are told, set very high stock by the power of education – and we cut to a shot of a crowded but jovial and multi-ethnic nursery. There's plenty of work – we are treated to a picture of a lowering Labour Exchange that looks more like a Victorian asylum – with pay of up to £9 or £10 a week. There is no evidence that this influx has caused unemployment among white workers. So, what's the problem?

Housing. Again. Lambeth's Mayor White is shown leading a delegation to the Colonial Office in Whitehall. There are 10,000 people on the waiting list in the borough. What is to be done? Given that the entire city of Birmingham was building houses, as we have seen, at the rate of 2,000 a year, the obvious answer of undertaking more construction was not the one at the top of Mayor White's list. What needed to be addressed was clear: interventions to ensure that social conditions in the West Indies could be improved so that the lure of the motherland would become less attractive.

It's unlikely that Mayor Major Herbert N White would have been the first to blow the dog-whistle of 'send them home' and, to be fair to him there was, as mentioned above, a strong belief among some in immigrant communities themselves that their stay would only be temporary. But the argument was being made with absolute clarity: if there is a shortage of housing, services and employment, it's because an 'other' is taking what is rightfully yours. Plenty of immigrants were, as we shall see, more than capable of understanding the force and effect of this specious suggestion. It is delusional for us in 2021 to imagine that the creation of a 'hostile environment', to which we will return in Chapter 11, is some kind of new phenomenon. Those in the first wave of migration immediately recognised the nagging chill of such hostility.

Thanks to the work of Black commentators, artists and academics, there is now a range of resources that can convey something of the shock encountered by the early arrivals from the Caribbean. One of the most recognisable of these voices belongs to the poet, Benjamin Zephaniah who was born in 1956 in Handsworth, north of Lee Bank, to a father hailing from Barbados and a mother from Jamaica. It was Handsworth rather than Balsall Heath, or those parts of Edgbaston that abutted the city centre, that became, as Zephaniah dubbed it, 'the Jamaican capital of Europe'. He captures the vitality and energy of the place in his poem *Soho Road Then and Now,* telling of how:

> *On Soho road from night to day*
> *From time to time come rain come shine*
> *We buy and sell, we wine and dine*
> *That's how we build a nation here*

Yet for all of this optimistic tone, he cannot avoid returning to one recurring theme in all the memoirs and accounts of the Windrush generation and their children: the weather. Handsworth may well have been bright and lively with the colours and smells reminiscent of a distant world, but it remained, in Zephaniah's words, 'a cold suburb of Kingston, Jamaica'. Grace Nichols, another poet with Caribbean roots in Guyana and a later immigrant to the UK, imagines an 'island man... groggily, groggily' awakening from a sleep infused with images of 'blue surf... wild seabirds' on 'a small emerald isle' to the grinding reality of a 'grey metallic soar' and the 'surge of wheels' on dull roads. More prosaically, a young Bill Morris arrived, aged 16, in Handsworth in 1954 to join his recently widowed mother. Later life saw him progress to become Britain's first Black leader of a major trade union – (the TGWU) – and eventually to take his place in the House of Lords, where he assumed the title of Baron Morris of Handsworth. Goodness only knows what earlier settlers in that part of the city would have made of that – and goodness only knows what Bill Morris would have made of his own union's Harry Green's comments about busmen back in 1955. On his arrival, however, a boy from the countryside trussed up in a suit, his abiding recollection is of a place that was 'cold, wet and grey' with 'boxes on roofs which smoked'; chimneys had not been a part of his life. He was still quietly nurturing his dream of one day returning home a richer man and playing cricket for the West Indies.

Three years earlier, another Jamaican from a different social background made his way to the UK. Stuart Hall was going to Merton College, Oxford, having gained a scholarship to study English. As he made his initial journey from Bristol to London, Hall recalls looking out of the train window to see the countryside that his imagination had conjured from the novels of Thomas Hardy, reinforcing the entrenched, romantic notions of England as the motherland. His studies and experiences took his thoughts down some very different routes and by 1964 he was instrumental in establishing the Centre of Contemporary Cultural Studies at the University of Birmingham. As one of the major intellectual movements of the latter part of the century, Hall and his colleagues at the Centre went on to analyse – and challenge – some of the basic notions of Black identity and experience of racism in modern Britain.

When Hall died in 2014 aged 82, he left a legacy of wide-ranging publications universally acknowledged as major contributions to the understanding of the experience of those who formed the Caribbean diaspora. Director John Akomfrah's film, *The Stuart Hall Project*, with a haunting soundtrack pieced together from the work of Miles Davis, is mandatory viewing for anyone requiring a comprehensive overview of the history, politics and lived experience of those whose history is rooted in the islands. Hall himself presented a critical view of that history in his seven-part TV series, *Redemption Song*, shown on BBC in 1991. His observation that 'those who do not see themselves reflected in national heritage are excluded from it' now underpins the thinking that manifested itself in a wider depiction of people of colour and their interests in popular culture which would have been unthinkable when he first arrived in England and for some tears thereafter.

Outside the city in Dudley, Lenny Henry was born to Jamaican immigrants in 1956, albeit not quite, as his memoirs explain, to the father he assumed to be his parent. In an affectionate dig at his Black Country neighbours which always raises a knowing smile from people from the region, his stage act often refers to trips to 'Burningham' when mimicking his own childhood voice. What is not quite so jolly is the account of the racism endured by his mother on a daily basis in the early 1960s. Local children would ask her where she kept her tail; women on the bus would wipe their hands across her face to see if the colour would come off; monkey noises from men in the street were common. And still, there was the weather: 'it was cold all the time, even when it was meant to be summer, and she never really got used to that'.

Plenty of documentary footage provides visual testament to the drabness of this withering climate, exacerbated by backdrops of grimy urban streets and houses. An abiding cliché of childhood memories is of never-ending, hazy summer days. Like many Brummies, my default position towards life, although fundamentally cheerful, is also informed by a stoic pessimism which means I am never shocked when things take a turn for the worse. That may account for my own recollections of the weather of my early years being dominated by the blight of thick fog and the insides of bedroom windows frozen into sharply spiked patterns at a time long before central heating. It may just be that two meteorological events, both occurring within weeks of the trial and execution of Oswald Grey, distorted these imaginings.

In December 1962, large parts of the country became suffocated by freezing fog, intensified, of course, by the mass of unregulated industrial waste that poured into the atmosphere. In a city where most people relied on public transport to get to work, it had a crippling effect. I remember my mother returning from her job in Bradford Street in the heart of the city's engineering industry, having had to walk half the way when the driver was forced to abandon his vehicle on the Alcester Road. On removing the scarf that she had wrapped around her mouth and nostrils as protection, it revealed a chin, lips and nostrils that were perfectly clean, in contrast to the rest of a face that looked as though she had just come up from a shift in a coal mine.

Unlike my recollection of the evening of Grey's execution, clear documentary evidence exists of this grimy climatological event. Writing in *The Journal of the Air Pollution Control Association* in 1963, Arnold Marsh analyses in great scientific detail the chemical composition of 'the great smog...which developed on Monday, December 3, 1962, and did not clear until the following Friday, affecting many parts of Britain'. According to his records, this particularly noxious event began somewhat earlier in Birmingham at the end of the previous week and that 'by December 8 the week's total of deaths from respiratory illness, 41, was the highest since the beginning of October'. If this was one of the more extreme episodes of the choking, blanketing fogs that were a part of life in industrial cities in the 1950s and 60s, the case of the great smog was merely a taster for something that has seen little to rival it for bitter, biting, prolonged cold weather since.

The winter of 1963 was relentless, both in Birmingham and across the country. Temperatures began to drop on the evening of Boxing Day, 1962 and there ensued ten to twelve weeks, depending on the exact location, of ice and snow that took a grip on all aspects of life. By 25 January, the *Birmingham Post* offered a ray of hope by reporting that the Meteorological Office had suggested 'that there is a good chance that the cold spell is beginning to end'. This was in the face of Edgbaston Observatory reporting overnight temperatures of minus 8.3 degrees and stories from elsewhere of parts of the sea turning to ice. The same front page informed readers of the National Coal Board arranging emergency drops of coal for domestic use and of how the weather had affected unemployment with a near record figure of 814,631 people registered nationally as being out of work.

The Post's hopeful predictions turned out to be over sanguine. It wasn't until 2 March when things had, at last, begun to ease a little, that the paper was able to take stock of the telling statistics for the area. According to the Edgbaston Observatory, in the three months since the start of January, there were 34 days when the temperature never rose above freezing all day. There were 36 days on which snow fell and 67 when snow covered over three-quarters of the ground. What these bald statistics do not reveal is the domestic misery caused in terms of the flooding caused by broken pipes even in homes, like my own, that were relatively comfortable by the standards of the time. The substandard accommodation and sparse lodging rooms of those still relatively new to Britain would have fared considerably worse. By now, a good many in the Jamaican community had come to terms with the fact that their migration was probably not a temporary interlude – and they must have thought that if they could endure the winter of 1963, they'd be able to put up with anything.

For all the depredations thrust on these new arrivals, those with the tense 'faces filled with hope and apprehension of the smartly dressed men in suits and fedoras disembarking from HMT Empire Windrush at Tilbury in 1948' as characterised in Colin Grant's compelling set of narratives in *Homecoming – Voices of the Windrush Generation*, there was joy and happiness to be gleaned. Grant recalls with deep pride the thrill of being part of something exotic in his home town, Luton, in the 1960s. 'Walking through the West Indian neighbourhoods,' he tells us, 'was like walking through the musical *Guys and Dolls*' populated by larger-than-life characters nicknamed Bageye (his dad), Tidy Boots, Shine, Pumpkin Head, Summer Wear and Pioneer. In Birmingham, where Oswald Grey knocked around with Hercules, Parchment and Mover, it was music that also reinforced a central part of the formation of this cultural identity, even though Black people often found the doors of mainstream venues closed to them in the early 1960s.

As a consequence, Black music in Birmingham in the 1960s moved into private houses where blues parties replicated the notion of the all-night communal tea-parties of rural Jamaica. Furniture was rearranged, payment was made at the door and the urban myth is that electricity for such events was always hijacked from local street lighting. In his film *Lovers Rock*, first broadcast in late 2020, director Steve McQueen lovingly replicates such an episode, albeit set some years later in the mid-1970s. The critic, Micha Frazer-Carroll, praised the authenticity of McQueen's portrayal – and she speaks from a position of some authority. In a central scene, the partygoers move dreamily into an almost ecstatic, unaccompanied rendition of the song *Silly Games*, something of a party staple. The singer, Janet Kay, was a family friend of Frazer-Carroll – an 'auntie' – and the song was also sung communally at other family gatherings such as communions and weddings. Frazer-Carroll explains that blues parties were 'places of celebration and togetherness – and crucially, the only place you could hear reggae and lovers rock' and praises McQueen's attention to detail. Her mother, however, was a touch more critical, taking issue with the accents and, as she saw it, the overly tactile dancing: 'the art was to dance as close as possible without touching'.

The historian of Black music, Carl Loben, sees a clear and obvious linkage between the early blues parties and their contemporary counterparts. The soundsystem culture, he suggests, had originated in Jamaica 'when DJs would load up a truck with a generator, turntables and huge speakers' and then that same DJ would 'rap' over the selected tunes. 'As time went on,' Loben explains, 'crews began cutting dubplates so that they'd have exclusive original sounds – a precursor to how drum and bass would operate decades later.'

For the main part, Black people enjoyed music and dance in private places – a situation that endured well into the 1980s, notwithstanding constant police harassment and the official disapproval of local authorities. It took until the end of the 60s for Birmingham's clubs and music locations to become more integrated in terms of the bands who performed there, if not necessarily in the make-up of the audience. In his book *Cut'n'Mix: Culture, Identity and Caribbean Music*, Dick Hebdige was able to write about how, by the end of the decade, Birmingham was 'one of the few places left in Britain where it's still possible for a white man to get into a shebeen without wearing a blue uniform and kicking the door down'. Such advances may well have been made and they certainly informed the folklore, if not the direct experience, of my own later teenage years. There seems little doubt, however, that such integration would have been a rarity on that June afternoon and evening when Oswald Grey seems to have drifted between Balsall Heath, Lee Bank and Lozells.

On TV, a feature in most homes by the early 1960s, Black faces were still a rarity. In my conversations when conducting research, I would frequently hear stories about family members being summoned to the telly because a Black person had appeared. Another version of blackness was, however, more readily available. On the evening of the murder of Thomas Bates, a programme missing on the TV schedule was the BBC 'favourite' *The Black and White Minstrel Show*. It was possibly enjoying a summer break, gearing itself up for returning in the autumn and its blockbuster Christmas special. With regular audiences of over 16 million, it won the prestigious Golden Rose of Montreux award in 1961. On a personal note, my loathing of it was deep and visceral, which was unfortunate as it was one of my mother's great pleasures. I'd like to be able to tell you that even at an early age, and with my own frequent encounters with antisemitic language and gestures, this antipathy was born of principle. That's not true: I just hated the songs and the dancing. Looking back at it now, one can only shudder at its racist nature, although it is gratifying to know that even in its heyday, the show faced opposition and opprobrium.

The BBC's chief accountant at the time, Barrie Thorne, had worked in the Corporation's New York office where he had become acquainted with the activities of the civil rights movements. He wrote to the Director-General, Hugh Greene, to counteract his assertion that the minstrels were nothing more than a part of a 'traditional show enjoyed by millions for what it offers in good-hearted family entertainment'. Dismissing this suggestion as something that may once have been said about throwing Christians to lions, Thorne goes on to argue that 'many regard the show as Uncle Tom from start to finish, and as such is underlyingly offensive to many, no matter what the outward gloss and size of audience prove to the contrary.' The written response, from Greene's assistant, Oliver Whitley, is startling. 'On this issue, we can see your point,' he concedes, 'but in your own interests, for Heaven's sake, shut up. You are wasting valuable ammunition on a comparatively insignificant target.' Even from a distance of nearly sixty years, it's easy to assume that a Saturday evening in with the telly would have had little appeal for Oswald or any of his circle.

The minstrels may have been an affront to people of Caribbean heritage, but cultural identity nurtured itself in another area of the lives of incomers from Jamaica – the church. Although most churches outwardly adhered to the properly Christian idea of welcoming the outsider, there is ample testimony that this was often more honoured in the breach than the observance. Bishop Dr Joe Aldred came to Birmingham from Jamaica in 1968 to join his father who had emigrated some years earlier. In the wonderfully illuminating BBC programme *The First Black Brummies*, he talks of how some not-so-subtle messages were often conveyed to worshippers who had ventured into places where they had assumed they would be welcome. Bishop Joe recalls with obvious dismay that Jamaican parishioners could not have failed to hear some of the stage whispers from congregants, suggesting that they would feel more comfortable hearing the word of the Lord among their own. Little wonder, therefore, that so many of them found a spiritual home in the early days of makeshift evangelical churches, where the style and manner of worship was more to their liking.

One of the leading figures of this movement in Birmingham was the Reverend, later Bishop, Sidney Dunn, whose energetic and passionate style is captured in the same film. Dunn, who died at 95 in 2017, was an extraordinary character in many ways. Apart from his challenging views on ecumenical matters, he once found himself, entirely innocently as it turns out, at the centre of an alarming scandal when, aged 77, a loyal parishioner was accused of hiring a hitman to dispose of the bishop whom he accused of sleeping with his wife. His preaching and religious conviction had great resonance with his growing congregations, with much talk of resilience inspired by faith, along with social and spiritual regeneration. As Bishop Joe wryly observes, 'Bishop Dunn would never have actually said that Jesus was Black, but he all but said so.' It must have been a message very happily received by so many of his followers negotiating a strange and often hostile world.

In February 2021, I Zoom call Bishop Joe who has recently retired from his official positions. In *Black Brummies* he had been at pains to point out that he regarded his family's move from the Caribbean to England as their second migration, the first being the displacement of their ancestors to Jamaica. This strong sense of history informs his analysis of his countrymen's relationship with the church, both when they arrived and in the succeeding decades. The animated Bishop Dunn may well have augmented his congregation from those disappointed with their welcome in the churches they found in their new home. Nevertheless, Bishop Joe maintains, the establishment of home-grown places and forms of worship were just as often an expression of self-reliance and independence, put into effect by people who brought some historical perspective to their actions and aspirations. 'If they'd read any history,' he tells me, 'they'd have known that an advert that told them to come to England wouldn't just wash away centuries' worth of mistreatment and prejudice.' This notion that rejection was not the driving force behind the actions of those setting up their own places of worship is significant. It stands as an early reminder that those attempting to set up new lives would not always do so in forms that could only be judged by their relationship to what already existed in the society in which they now found themselves.

There was one other area of life that afforded the Caribbean diaspora joy and pride: their prowess at cricket. The place of the game in the consciousness of so many from that part of the world is difficult to overstate, especially when viewed from a time dominated by global, marketized models of franchised sport. In his seminal account of cricket and society, C L R James – 'what do they know of cricket who only cricket know' – captures the pre-eminence of cricket in his native Trinidad. He grew up in a place where, he tells us, 'recreation meant cricket, for in those days...cricket was the only game.' Some forty years later, his nephew, the writer and campaigner, Darcus Howe, imbued the game with an even greater significance.

The British ruled these islands, dominated the natives with the explicit belief that we deserve slavery and colonialism because we are an inferior people. The masters brought the game to the island, taught us its complexities and nuances and a victory over the English has always been savoured with that taste for revenge. It is so; it has always been so.

Early arrivals in the late 1940s who possessed the means to follow the game would have been delighted when the West Indies team came to England in 1950 and decisively defeated their hosts in a series of matches. Writing in 1990, recalling the second game in the series at Lord's, the very bastion of English cricket, John Arlott called the event 'the first truly bipartisan Test match' and of how 'it was amazing to see the number of West Indian spectators'. England's followers 'had never known such a jolly atmosphere at cricket matches' and were 'carried away by the carefree, purposeful cricket of the visitors'.

Almost all of whom were Black with one of the few exceptions being the captain, John Goddard. It was not until 1960 that the West Indies cricket authorities felt confident enough – or could no longer ignore the manifold pressures upon them – to appoint a Black captain; Frank, later to be Sir Frank Worrell.

In 1963, with the fogs, ice and snow of the previous winter fading in the memory, Worrell brought his team of dashing batsmen and fearsome fast bowlers, now a genuine force in world cricket, to England and inflicted another defeat on hosts who looked hopelessly out of their depth playing the game the English had brought to the world, but the development of which was rapidly passing them by. The West Indies won the series 3-1, with England's sole victory coming at Edgbaston in early July – just over a year since Thomas Bates might have saved himself by going to the county ground as his brother expected him to do. Oswald Grey's lodgings in Cannon Hill Road were no more than a five-minute stroll to the ground, but given that, as we shall see, we are able to glean so little secure knowledge about him, it is impossible to know whether he would ever have been interested enough to stroll round the corner to enjoy a few hours' cricket.

If Birmingham's Jamaican community was unable to enjoy victory at first-hand, they would have enjoyed the TV pictures a month or so later when people of Caribbean descent streamed across the playing surface at The Oval in London to celebrate a crushing victory and a series win. They and their offspring were about to experience three decades during which their team rose to dominate the world game, to the obvious irritation of racist politicians like Norman Tebbit who, in 1990, challenged immigrant communities to abandon their allegiance to the teams of their heritage as a way of showing their full integration. For Jamaicans in particular, the fierce and proud future exploits of Michael Holding, Courtney Walsh and Chris Gayle went on to serve as sufficient riposte to such nonsense.

Music, Saturday night, church and cricket provided much-needed balm to working days and weeks that were long, demanding and often physically punishing. Many in Birmingham's new communities looked beyond these welcome diversions and worked hard to make sense of their situation.

Philip Donnellan's 1964 film *The Colony* (also featuring some early, fiery Sidney Dunn) shows an immensely thoughtful Stan Crooke, a sanitary inspector in his native St Kitts but now working as a railwayman, trying to steer some companions towards a considered analysis of what they expected from integration. In the later *Black Brummies*, his son, Earl, ruefully muses on the fact that he wasn't sure that his parents had ever been guests in a white household and that such separation would have been the norm. With casual day-to-day racism, discrimination and isolation, even from those organisations that should have been reliable sources of support, inclement weather in draughty, substandard accommodation and a festering political discourse unwilling to challenge prejudice and inequality, life in the early 1960s must have felt fragile and uncomfortable.

The Colony provided one of the few cultural manifestations that gave access to unmediated Black voices in the early days of mass immigration. There was, however, another rather disturbing instance where it seemed as though another pathway might have emerged, but all was not as it appeared. In September 1961 a new, glossy magazine, *Flamingo*, could be purchased for 1 shilling and 6 pence (about 7p). Replicas can be examined at the online archives of the British Library. Its initial editorial makes its intentions very clear:

> *Some people in Britain – and I'm referring to those afflicted with the disease of race prejudice – resent the fact that there 350,000 West Indians and many thousands of Africans and Asians now living here. But it is a fact that these West Indians, Africans and Asians are as much a part of the British scene as the Welsh, the Scots and the Irish. Up until now, the Negro citizens of Britain have been denied a Voice.*

It is this voice, significantly capitalised and a prescient prophecy of one of the strongest mouthpieces of Black Britain – *The Voice*

– that *Flamingo* promises to provide. The pages that follow feature articles that are determinedly positive and which mix the global with the local with the domestic. Pieces feature the Black proprietor of a taxi firm, advice on homemade winemaking and the fight against a newly confident National Front. It's an eclectic and fascinating collection and one that speaks of a community attempting to establish itself in a range of society's mores and expectations. All of which make recent revelations about its provenance something of a disappointment.

Once *Flamingo* became established, it sold around 20,000 copies each month until its final edition in May 1965. It had some international distribution and once enjoyed a major scoop by interviewing Malcolm X. It energetically promoted Island Records, thus enabling Ska music to become available to a wider British audience. And its founder was an M16 intelligence officer whose brief was to ensure that it was used to push an anti-communist agenda among Black and West Indian communities.

That founder, Peter Hornsby, died in 2000 and some years later his widow, Jennifer, disclosed this information, which was part of his collected memoirs, to researcher and academic, Stephen Dorril. Her husband's intentions, according to her, were entirely honourable, informed by a desire to promote social integration and acceptance. There was, however, no escaping the reason why one of the state's most intrusive scrutineers might be entangled with such a journal. 'There were people inside MI6,' explains Dorril, 'who saw which way Africa was going in terms of politics and nationalism, and were willing to support Black students, writers and aspiring politicians who were on the left but who could be persuaded to oppose communism.' Jennifer Hornsby displays obvious loyalty: 'in Peter's mind, a magazine focusing on immigrants would make them feel welcome and ease their integration into British society,' she told *The Observer* newspaper. Nevertheless, it seems that those arriving from Jamaica and elsewhere were to be protected in their new homeland from evil influence. A less charitable interpretation suggests the beginnings of the deep-seated mistrust that became characteristic of the way in which Britain's establishment viewed society's newcomers.

This chapter has tried to sketch something of the backdrop against which Oswald Grey's time in Birmingham was played out. Piecing together the details of his life is, as we shall discover, a demanding and sometimes frustrating business and what is written here is remembered, selected and painted by a white man from sixty years' distance – and one in whose ears Chinua Achebe's famous quotation has been ringing constantly: 'until the lions have their own historians then the story of the hunt will always glorify the hunter'.

As I put this picture together, as I listened to some people and read the words of others, as I heard them express their thoughts on film and looked through documentation, a nagging thought persisted. Music, church, cricket, despair about life-deadening weather and the beginnings of the notions of resistance and collective organisation, all formed part of the collective consciousness of those whose roots were elsewhere. Beyond these factors, their existences were bound together by one, all-consuming common factor: the central importance of work. It was through work that immigrants defined themselves, their place in society and their relationships. Account after account about Black people's experience in the 1950s and 60s, irrespective of the context, begins by them defining themselves in terms of how they made their living: 'I was a civil engineer at home but went to London Transport and went to night school to get my certificates'; 'my mum worked as a nurse and she met my dad who was a hospital porter'; 'my husband hated his factory job and walked out – then he got a job as a guard on the railways'. Such testimony is ubiquitous. There was discrimination in terms of pay and conditions and there were incessant racist jibes – but work was readily available.

In a parliamentary debate about rising regional unemployment at the very end of 1962, Hansard reports that a mere 2% of industrious Birmingham's population was out of work. One of these was Oswald Grey. Out of work when jobs were plentiful and sliding into a life of petty crime – a dispiriting picture of a young man who was obviously floundering as he tried to make his mark in a chilly, foreign land. And, having failed to make any such mark during his brief life, he has, until now, been condemned to his memory being deemed equally insignificant. I am trying to put that right.

Chapter 5

The official details - still firmly locked in the vault.

The main principle behind freedom of information legislation is that people have a right to know about the activities of public authorities, unless there is a good reason for them not to. This is sometimes described as a presumption or assumption in favour of disclosure.
From the website of the Information Commissioner's Office.

The court papers relating to the trial and conviction of Oswald Augustus Grey in October 1962 reside in the National Archive at Kew: the index number for the trial documents is 2/3485. Those relating to his brief appeal later that month are located in the same place, indexed as 2/3556. In early October 2020, I began the process of requesting access to them by submitting a request as permitted by Freedom of Information legislation.

There was nothing to indicate that this would be a controversial request. First, it was nearly sixty years since the murder of Thomas Bates. He was unmarried and had no children. Those relatives alive at the time, his brother and his mother, are long dead. It is feasible that some witnesses and jury members may still be alive sixty years on and it may be that any revival of the event through my intended account could be painful for them. However, in my convoluted dealings with the National Archive and the Freedom of Information Commissioner's Office over the next year, I made it clear that my intention was to produce an authoritative, transparent account of events, not least in an attempt to dispel and deflate some of the more lurid and speculative versions that were in the public domain.

The Freedom of Information (FOI) Act of 2000 was introduced by the government of Tony Blair who had come to office in

1997. It was intended as a clear sign that these were different days and that the fusty, secretive world of entitled legislators and clubbable, drunk-in-the-afternoon executives would now be open to clear-eyed public scrutiny. Individuals and organisations would have access to documentation that revealed the deliberations and decision-making of those whose actions impacted on public health and welfare. It was a bold step, but it didn't take long for the sheen of this promise to tarnish.

By 1999, Blair had already informed the British Venture Capitalists Association that he bore 'the scars on my back' of trying to reform public services, thereby beginning the process of alienating millions who voted for him. By the time he had comprehensively completed this project through his support for the Iraq war and his shows of contempt for the history and traditions of the labour movement, Blair was berating himself for his error of judgement in supporting the Act. In his memoirs, he calls himself a 'naive, foolish, irresponsible nincompoop' for backing it. It had not, he moaned, signalled 'a new relationship between government and people' which would see the public as legitimate stakeholders in the running of the country'. Instead, it had become a weapon to be used 'not by the people' but by journalists and researchers.

He was not alone in his despair. David Cameron called the act a 'buggeration' and 'clutteration' of government. By the time Michael Gove, who had acted as education secretary through most of Cameron's time as Prime Minister, assumed responsibility for the Cabinet Office, it was clear that antipathy towards the Act had become deeply imprinted onto the minds of governments of all stripes. In February 2021, it came to light, through the doggedness of those very journalists of whom Blair and Cameron were so fretfully suspicious, that Gove was presiding over a shady set-up, known in the Cabinet Office as Clearing House. Its brief appeared to be to deter applications for information, identifying troublesome applicants and placing them on a blacklist.

Editors and owners of British newspapers of all political persuasions wrote to the Cabinet Office demanding an investigation into Clearing House, which, at the time of writing remains unanswered. Their concerns were given substance by some revealing data. In the decade to 2019, the number of requests for information granted in full fell from 62% to 42%. Flat denials of access rose from 21% to 35%. In the same period, funding for the Information Commissioner's Office suffered a cut of 41% in real terms. Journalist and campaigner, Peter Geoghehan, characterises the situation as one where 'rather than trying to legislate to get rid of it, which generates headlines, you have government starving FOI'. Campaigner and journalist Lucas Amin wrote about the prevalence of the delay, stonewalling, schoolboy tactics and procedure errors which bedevil many FOI requests. My own twelve-month wrangle with the system bears out this judgement entirely. The Act has clearly become an unwanted, ugly baby – an embarrassment to its political parents and wider family.

A sense of perspective needs to be maintained here. I want to be unambiguous about my experience of navigating a system that has honed its ability to obfuscate and obstruct to the level of high art. I am not attempting to get to the root cause of why people died at Grenfell Tower because of negligent inefficiency; I am not searching for information from Alder Hey Hospital relating to infant mortality. I make no claim that my curiosity about an event from 60 years ago, notwithstanding its current resonance with issues about continuing racism and discrimination, carries an immediate or current moral equivalence. Nevertheless, since early October 2020 when I attempted to invoke FOI to see the papers relating to the trial and subsequent appeal of Oswald Augustus Grey, a digitally reinforced, bureaucratic force-field has been put into place, deftly and disingenuously deflecting any attempt to gain access. Had these obstructive devices not been so frustrating, there might even have been a funny side.

A succession of automated responses from the National Archive replete with baffling sequences of sentences plucked from a statement bank – something made even more obvious by inaccurate punctuation and random capitalisation of the text – found their way to my inbox. In fairness, it is possible that those charged with running their offices at Kew may have wished to keep numbers using the facility to a bare minimum during the Covid pandemic and such clumsy communication reflected this. Eventually, however, I received an initial decision.

Some four months after the first request and after much prompting and 'reminding' on my part, I was notified that my request to see papers relating to the trial had been refused on two grounds. First, I was advised that 'there is a profound public interest in not endangering the mental health of the defendant's remaining family members'. Second, 'the defendant's surviving family members would not have knowledge that these details would be put in the public domain after such a significant amount of time'. I was advised of my right to ask for a review from the Information Commissioner's Office and that is something I undertook forthwith.

My argument rested on three propositions. First, it was difficult to imagine that the mental health of any surviving family members, who had already experienced shame and trauma some sixty years ago, could be further endangered by an authoritative, fully informed account of what had taken place. Second, given the haphazard and sometimes lurid material available about Grey's crime, his demise and that of Thomas Bates, access to official material could provide reliable and convincing accounts to counteract the prevailing inaccuracies and calumnies referred to in the next chapter. Finally, as will be revealed, relatives of Grey or his father have become all but untraceable. I also chanced the argument that the investigation of a forgotten Black life in current societal circumstances had, in itself, a certain moral imperative. On reflection, introducing that last notion may have been a tactical error, given the inclination towards denial of requests underpinned by the manoeuvrings of Clearing House.

In mid-April 2021, I was pleasantly surprised to hear from the Information Commissioner's Office that my case had 'been accepted as eligible for further consideration and will be allocated to a case officer as soon as possible'. Less encouraging was the fact that this officer would be assigned to me in approximately six months time. As it turned out, the process was quicker than this and in September 2021, I received a full and comprehensive report from the office of the Information Commissioner. If that was the good news, the bad news was that, despite the force of my arguments, clearly and graciously acknowledged by the Commissioner, the decision of the National Archive not to release the trial and appeal papers was upheld.

The original judgement by the National Archive was that allowing access to material ending up in the public domain could 'endanger the physical or mental health of any individual' or 'endanger the safety of any individual'. The argument that the number of any survivors likely to be around and prone to such danger would be minimal is superseded by the '100-year principle'. Under this principle, anyone person connected to the case born later than 1921 is presumed to be living. The judgement cites the possibility of Thomas Bates's nephews falling into this category as well as any siblings of Oswald Grey. Intriguingly, and frustratingly, the Commissioner's report suggests that the court papers may throw some light on the existence of such individuals. Although she concedes that the '100-year principle is a cautious one' and that extensive research has been undertaken to locate anyone connected to the episode, in order to be sure that the principle is not infringed, what is required is 'evidence to ascertain the death of an individual such as death certificates, published obituaries or entries in official histories'.

I was granted the right to one further legal appeal, but given that this could take years to reach court, it was one that I chose to forgo.

And so the official record of the brief trial, briefer appeal and peremptory conviction of Oswald Augustus Grey in the autumn of 1962 sits guarded and unobtainable in a vault in Kew. Any light that it may have shed on Oswald, his father, Felix, or the acquaintances they kept remains dimmed. Any illumination of attitudes from the constabulary, the judiciary or those who bore witness or deliberated as jurors remains stubbornly dim.

By strange contrast, the National Archive allows free access to secret minutes of Cabinet meetings held during the weeks of the trial. Details of the deliberations over rail workers' wages, judges' pensions and the possibility of joining the European common market are freely available. Concerns about wealth and population growth are captured in the note that 'if new policies were not put in hand at an early date, there was a danger of the country being split between a prosperous South and a relatively stagnant North'. Ministers are informed that the Prime Minister had spoken to President Kennedy about his intention to invade Cuba and that the President 'had reiterated his view that firmness offered the best chance of avoiding the outbreak of a third world war and had recalled the lesson of Hitler'.

All of this and more is in the public domain and easily accessible. The notes covering what happened in the few hours it took to dispense justice to a Black boy in Birmingham at exactly the same time remain resolutely unreachable. What follows in the next chapter, therefore, is the best version of events that can be furnished about a forgotten tragedy.

Chapter 6

Arrest, trial and conviction. Why a bewildered Oswald never stood a chance.

Thirty years after the execution of Oswald Grey, the senior detective whose investigation had helped to condemn him, George Baumber, died at the age of 76. As with Grey, you have to scroll down a fair number of entries to find him on an internet search: neither man has made a permanent stamp on history. Baumber suffered the further indignity of lazy sub-editors frequently misspelling his name when transcribing their lines from various press agencies, but one imagines this would have been of little concern to him as he successfully set about his professional business. He may, however, have been a little miffed at the somewhat low-key coverage of his efforts, especially in the local press where he might have expected a bit more of a splash.

Following the initial reports of the murder, along with tales of the trawling of the number 8 bus and the observations of 10-year-old Ann Bradley, more details found their way into the papers. The most widespread coverage was, unsurprisingly, in the *Birmingham Post*, but it is an extraordinary fact – at least to modern observers – that from the moment of the murder of Thomas Bates until the execution of Oswald Grey, that newspaper, and indeed no other, ever made it headline news. For the most part, the coverage of the search for a culprit, Grey's trial, his conviction, appeal (especially the appeal) and execution, nestled among the localised and banal and was rarely afforded more than two columns. And even when making allowances for different times, it was shot through with naked racism.

'Police seek slit-eyed man' was the by-line in the *Belfast Telegraph* two days after the murder on 4 June. According to their interpretation, the suspect was 'coloured, between 30 and 40, about five feet eight inches tall, slim build, prominent cheek bones and long slit eyes'. The next day, he had transformed a little according to the *Birmingham Post*. He was now between 20 and 30 and although still around five feet eight inches, he had 'very black skin, broad build, upright stance ... (a) round face and wide nostrils'. It appeared that he was also something of a dandy, sporting a 'dark grey or green Robin Hood type hat with a feather at the side, a knee-length loose fitting overcoat of small black and white checks, narrow blue jeans with wide turnups and winkle-picker type shoes'.

Possibly inspired by this detailed description, Baumber and his team set to their task with a will. According to the *Post*, 100 officers had been assigned to the case with a brief to visit 'areas of the city inhabited by coloured people'. By the Wednesday – 6 June – expertise had been requisitioned from police forces from Manchester and Liverpool 'because of their special knowledge of coloured people'.

Whether it was this extra insight, a tip-off or even, perhaps, a chance sighting on a number 8 bus that paid dividends, Baumber's team was confident enough to arrest Grey at his lodgings on Cannon Hill Road on 6 June. He was found to be in possession of ammunition – one report suggested that police arrived just as he was emptying this into a dustbin – although it was not specified whether this was of the 7.6 mm variety that had killed Thomas Bates. Grey denied possession of any weapon, but it was from this point that his conflicting versions of events began the twists and turns that ultimately failed to convince jury and judge and sent him to the gallows.

He told the police that he had, indeed, once been in possession of a gun which he had stolen from the home of Harold Bacchus in Varna Road (which I must have walked past on any number of occasions). However, he no longer had the weapon because he had thrown it into the canal. Whether through coercion, confusion or just plain fear, Grey almost immediately changed his story and told Baumber's team that the gun was hidden in the flat of a friend he identified as Parchment, who lived in Albert Street, Lozells. Grey claimed that he had stayed the night there after a party on the evening of Bates's murder. Grey went with Baumber and his team to the house where they discovered the weapon in a wardrobe. Parchment denied all knowledge of it and Grey admitted concealing it there.

On Friday, 8 June, the papers were reporting on the previous day's appearance in Birmingham Assizes of Oswald Grey on the charges of stealing an automatic pistol – a Walther 7.65 mm automatic – and being in possession of 28 rounds of ammunition. Grey was reported as lodging in Cannon Hill Road, Edgbaston (just across the road from the county ground) and as being an unemployed baker. And being Jamaican. From that point, nearly every reference to him in every newspaper refers to him as such. With our knowledge of the British state's haphazard and unreliable dealings with the rights and citizenship of the Windrush generation and their descendants, it is unsurprising that both Oswald and his father, Felix, lived in this state of semi-citizenship. Official paperwork about either of them is scant. The notion of being Black British was still a distant chimera. Oswald Grey was Jamaican.

Just in case the good people of Birmingham needed reminding of his heritage, its local paper furnished them with a direct quotation from the accused when he was first charged on that Friday after the murder. In an initial hearing that lasted only a few minutes, he told the court that 'I steal revolver, but I did not shoot anyone.' He was then remanded in custody and appeared very briefly in court four weeks later charged with capital murder. There was no further press coverage of either the case or the investigation until his trial started at Birmingham Assizes on Monday 8 October, 128 days after the death of Thomas Bates.

Proceedings started unpromisingly for Oswald Grey according

to reports of his first day in court. On page 5 of the *Post*, under the headline 'Jamaican baker denies murder', the paper reported that Mr Graham Swanwick, QC, prosecuting, was able to claim that four people had positively identified Grey 'as somebody who was loitering suspiciously near the shop between 5.15 and 6 p.m. that evening'. According to the barrister, one of those witnesses would testify to seeing Grey looking into the Black and White café nearby at 4 o'clock and another to the fact that he had already been into Bates's shop at about 6 p.m. and had come out 'behaving very strangely'. Swanwick told the court that Grey was desperate for money and living on National Assistance. An empty cash box had been recovered at the scene of the crime, although Swanwick refrained from mentioning any proof to confirm that Grey had suddenly become flush with ready money after the event. The prosecutor conceded that there were no eyewitnesses to the murder which took place some thirty minutes later, as confirmed by the fact that Thomas's brother, John, left the premises just as the day's play finished at the cricket. Nevertheless, the weight of evidence against Grey was, he argued, overwhelming. Beginning on the afternoon of 8 October and running into the next day's proceedings, Swanwick appeared to revel in his role as he entertained the court with his dissection of Grey's chaotic claims about his movements and actions on the afternoon and evening of 2 June.

At first, he attested that he has spent the afternoon with a friend called Errol Thomas, known more widely as Hercules. Grey had then admitted that this was untrue and that he had been in Pious's café on Mary Street – a claim denied by the joint owners, both of whom were familiar with him as a regular customer. Their denial was particularly damning for Grey because he claimed that it was in the café that he had sold the stolen pistol to a friend known as Mover, whose real name was Harris Karnfi. He, in his turn, could provide no cover for Grey, claiming to have spent the entire day with his friend, Valerie Dolores and her sister Barbara, from 11 in the morning until 10 in the evening. To make matters worse, Karnfi denied Grey's claim that, having purchased or borrowed the pistol from Grey – the status of the exchange was unclear – he then returned it to him that evening at the party in Parchment's flat. The testimony from Grey's father, Felix, that he had been having a drink with him at the time of the murder, along with a friend, Phyllis Shields, at a time and place that none of the parties involved could specifically recall, was, according to Swanwick, incontrovertible proof that Grey was a liar and entirely untrustworthy.

On Thursday, 11 October press reports seemed to offer a glimmer of hope for the accused. On that day, page 7 of the *Post's* sported the headline 'Accused man was 'not the one I saw'. Margaret Jean Brownley 'a young nursery nurse' told the court of how, at about 6.40, she had heard a noise that she assumed to be a car backfiring. She then saw a man who had his back to her with his hand on the shop door, who then turned and ran down the Bristol Road. 'He was either a very dirty white man or a pale coloured man. His hair was long and straight and he had a sallow complexion.' She then looked at Grey and said that he was not that man.

Margaret's evidence was less compelling than it first appeared. In his cross-examination, Swanwick pointed out that her description corresponded with that of a Mr Cleghorn who had, indeed, run off towards the Bristol Road to phone for an ambulance. Swanwick then asked Mr Cleghorn to stand and for her to consider the proposition that he was, in fact, the man she had seen. While agreeing that there were clear similarities, Margaret was adamant that Cleghorn was not the man seen by her on Lee Bank Road that evening. The *Post* leaves it there before dealing with the defence's summing up in this perfunctory way: 'Mr James pointed out the inconsistencies in the statements of the various prosecution witnesses and the wide variation of the descriptions of the clothes the accused man was alleged to have been wearing at the time of the murder'. Mr Swanwick, we were told, would deliver his final address on the following day, Friday 12 October.

Which he duly did, recapping the inconsistencies in Grey's character and restating the unworthiness of his character and that of his known associates. Having done so, for the first time since the murder of Thomas Arthur Bates, court proceedings succeeded in pushing the news of the event onto the front page of the local paper. 'Death Sentence on Jamaican' nestled halfway down the page, just underneath the news that an angler had been fined £10 for striking a boy with whom he had lost his temper. The national papers deemed the matter of no interest, with the *Daily Mirror* reporting on a more lurid murder of 'beloved 73-year-old Mary O'Donnell' a purveyor of religious memorabilia in Clerkenwell – 'the Holy Lady of London's Little Italy'. The *Daily Herald* chose to revel in a 'midnight siege at Monte Carlo' as French authorities attempted to get Prince Rainier of that 'pocket principality' to pay some taxes, alongside the serious business of sneering at the appointment of Selwyn Lloyd by the Tories as the man to guide them to their next election victory – which, spoiler alert, he failed to do.

The *Birmingham Post* stayed with its local scandal, albeit in a noticeably low-key way. Swanwick had delivered his final summation, the jury had deliberated, reaching a verdict in less than an hour and Mr Justice Paull had imposed the ultimate sentence all within a working day. An execution date of 30 October at 8.00 a.m. – squeezing in the three Sundays required by law – was set. His defence counsel gave immediate notice of intention to appeal.

A tiny news snippet appears next to this report in *The Birmingham Post*. As a fleeting glimpse at a different era, albeit from a geographical distance, it is compelling in both its content and brevity. Here it is in its entirety, a telling footnote to the times in which Oswald Grey lived:

Colour Bar Broken
*A negro girl was enrolled at Patrick Henry College, Martinsville,
Virginia yesterday, the first negro to do so. She visited the college
when no classes were being held and registered without incident.*

The press had succeeded in constructing a narrative of sorts.
At times it was as jumbled and contradictory as Oswald Grey's
own version of events. Even allowing for the unknowing,
dismissive racism of the times, there is little doubting the
underlying discourse that mirrors the address made to the jury
by the prosecutor, Graham Swanwick, referred to in Chapter
2, in which he presents the picture of people living in a world
of dives, nightclubs and illicitly acquired weapons. Swanwick
doesn't quite refer to them as 'these people', but the implication
is not far from the surface.

There are obvious shortcomings to the press coverage.
Nevertheless, to look back at the printed media of 1962, even
at its most lurid end – and the *Birmingham Post* existed at some
distance from that – is to be impressed by an overall seriousness
that is distant from its modern counterpart. Two examples serve
to illustrate this.

First, front pages, even those of tabloid newspapers, consisted
of dense, tightly presented print. At the red-top end, this print
was embellished by pictures – in black and white – but never
to the extent of completely dominating the page. At the more
serious end, such illustration is rare. Although deemed by some
as sensationalist at the time, to modern sensibilities, the coverage
of events is positively decorous.

Second, papers with local-sounding titles from Aberdeen to
Bristol to Liverpool to Birmingham, bore no relation whatsoever
to anything currently referencing a locality on its masthead.
Headlines in these publications saw part of their brief as dealing
with matters of national and international import: there wasn't
a mayor opening a fete or a tree trunk that looked like Jesus

to be seen. They were reflective of a more sombre, deferential age, so beloved of modern mimics, keen to parody the plummy voices heard in radio news broadcasts and cinema newsreels. As another example, to watch the early TV interviews of politicians – usually one senior white man to another, both wreathed in cigarette smoke – is to be taken aback by both the civility and the gravity of the exchanges.

Press reporting in the 1960s may well have been a very different enterprise from its looser, more cavalier manifestation of more than a half a century later, but crime reporting has always generated a set of expectations from a readership eager for a glimpse into a world that is close to, yet different from, its own. We remain fascinated by the juxtaposition of the outlandish in our familiar surroundings. Modern TV reporters still clamour to find the classic interview with the murderer's neighbour: 'a nice, quiet bloke – always helped the woman opposite with her bins'. I acknowledge an irony that is not lost on me: a murder around the corner from where I went to school; the blood-stained man; the number 8 bus; he should have been at the cricket. Still haunting me after all these years. Fascinated by extraordinary events in ordinary surroundings.

But even allowing for a more solemn approach to news coverage, the papers of the day needed to make this clumsy, bungled, unglamorous episode into a drama of sorts for a readership comprising people like Louisa Bates, who might well have been looking forward to the courtroom drama of *Perry Mason* on the evening of her son's murder. Possibly relying on the old adage of the paper being tomorrow's chip wrapping, there was a tendency to be inconsistent and occasionally contradictory when it came to detail. Names are often misspelt; yesterday's inaccurate assertions are never corrected. The owners of Pious's café are recorded, probably transcribed as heard, as Cephas Smith and Mae Effie Dora Rose who would have been Sefus Smith and Effedora Rose who married some eighteen months later. Given that there were four people who failed to pick out Grey in an identity parade, the report that Graham Swanwick claimed the opposite to be true looks careless. Swanwick himself – whose life and tastes will be revealed in the following chapter – obviously cut a more dashing and reportable figure than his counterpart, Mr A. E. James QC, whose only mark of record in his career is to have served as the principal investigator into improper behaviour by a Detective Sergeant in the Met in 1964. Running through the coverage, there is a quietly disdainful and unsympathetic acceptance that there was little to doubt of this young Jamaican's guilt.

To restate the point, the possible crimes and execution of Oswald Grey barely made an impact when they occurred. As an entirely unscientific aside, in the year during which I was writing this book, I spoke to scores of people but encountered barely anyone I know to have been alive at the time, and thus potentially aware of the events, who has anything other than the blurriest of memories of this episode.

There is a handful of contributions, but no more than that, on Facebook and social media platforms, including commentary from people with a range of hazy recollections. A junior policeman at the time suggests that Grey was located as quickly as he was because of the intervention of an aggrieved informant, named elsewhere as local prostitute, Cecilia Gibbs. A poster claiming to be the son of the barber at Winson Green Prison recalls that his father told him of cutting Grey's hair while the prisoner was constantly crying and proclaiming his innocence – a claim his father firmly believed. Elsewhere, someone recalls being regularly sent to buy cigarettes from Bates's shop – Park Drive brand – and of Thomas Bates being a widely liked 'nice man', a character trait mentioned elsewhere in press reports. One contributor with vague childhood memories suggests that there could have been a major miscarriage of justice and maybe someone should make a film about it. The comment sits unanswered.

The most unsettling detail to emerge from the little that is written about Oswald Augustus Grey emerges from the writing of Stewart McLaughlin, the biographer of hangman Harry Allen. In the chapter which includes Grey's crime and execution, written in 2008, McLaughlin writes that 'Oswald Grey is said to have spent his last six weeks on earth limbo-dancing and hand-jiving in the death cell, apparently oblivious to his fate'. Given that McLaughlin was not serving at Winson Green at the time and that Robert Douglas, who was, fails to mention this detail, it is baffling to consider where this disturbingly stereotypical image comes from. Douglas, as we saw in Chapter 2, was capable of unrepentant racism of his own. Just as alarmingly, it is a detail repeated, unattributed and uncorroborated, in the May 2020 edition of *True Crime, Detective Monthly*. That periodical must have gone to print a few weeks prior to the death of George Floyd, but it's hard to argue against the notion that its editors, in repeating this unsubstantiated claim, seem to be stuck in the same unenlightened ground of the worst hacks of the 1960s.

On Monday 29 October 1962, just over two weeks from his conviction and sentencing, Grey's case went to the Court of Appeal, presided over by Justices Gorman, Salmon and Lord Chief Justice Lord Parker. It was the latter, having considered the case before the weighty Justices, who was charged with delivering the final condemnation. As with Swanwick's evidence at Birmingham Assizes, when considering Parker's judgements it is impossible to avoid the conclusion that it was the man (or, rather, a confused boy) and his character that was being judged, not the assessment of evidence that should have been cast-iron and incontrovertible before sending him to his death. Grey had, according to Parker, offered no fewer than five conflicting versions of his actions on the day of the murder and about the theft of the weapon. He had relied on the evidence of untrustworthy witnesses; Harris Karnfi in particular was 'a man of bad character'. His own father had clearly lied to the court.

There had been no conceivable misdirection from trial judge, Justice Paull, to the jury. The conviction was sound and execution was now set for Tuesday 20 November, dutifully observing the three-Sunday stipulation.

The balance of probabilities suggests that Oswald Augustus Grey killed Thomas Bates. Yet if we're talking about probabilities, it is more than likely that, once arrested, he found himself in a situation that he must have found confusing and intimidating. It is probable that he was assigned legal assistance that was not as energetic as it could have been when it came to preventing him from being killed by the state. A trial lasting less than a working week, a deliberation by a jury lasting less than an hour and an appeal hearing done and dusted in a day suggest the probability of an unwillingness to consider alternative narratives and explanations. The balance of probabilities should not have been sufficient grounds on which to endorse the legal decision to kill a man.

The chapters that follow continue a narrative that explores the factors militating against the fairness and even-handedness that Grey should have been afforded. It starts by looking at his chief prosecutor and what we can learn about different lives lived in the same country.

Chapter 7

Not like us. Other people with their guns, drugs and sex.

The development and maintenance of every culture requires the existence of another different and competing alter ego. The construction of identity ... involves establishing opposites and **otherness** *whose actuality is always subject to the continuous interpretation and reinterpretation of their differences from* **us**
Edward Said in *Orientalism* 1978

When Graham Swanwick QC evoked the world of errant Jamaicans as he went about the business of sending Oswald Grey to the gallows, he conjured for the jury a world of moral laxity and feeble submission to the temptations of the flesh. It was a world that displayed an infirmity of purpose when it came to proper expectations of treading an honest path through life. Swanwick talked of guns, nightclubs, loose women and the use of intoxicating substances. This 'strange world' of gun-stealers and their 'aimless lives in night-clubs and dives,' he told the jury, was one that was alien to us. Whether or not it was such *terra incognita* for the twelve good men and true, will remain unknown. One thing is for certain. As far as Graham Swanwick was concerned, whatever universe was inhabited by Oswald Grey and his acquaintances, it certainly wasn't one familiar to him: or, as Said, would have observed, to *us*.

Swanwick died peacefully in his bed in 2003 aged 96. By then he was Sir Graham and a former High Court judge. He had been educated at Winchester and Oxford before going on to serve with distinction in the RAF during the war. He was awarded a military MBE and was mentioned in dispatches. He merited lengthy obituaries in all the broadsheet newspapers, all of which focussed on his part in the prosecution of Hanratty as well as his involvement in the trial of those taking part in The Great Train Robbery in 1963. He was, apparently, a man who delighted in country pursuits (in the literal, non-Shakespearean sense) and, according to the *Guardian's* tribute was someone who 'had not always endeared himself to his fellow judges on the circuit when they found they were sharing lodgings with him and his dogs'. Unsurprisingly, there was no mention anywhere of the breezy, professional confidence which he brought to his part in the despatch of an unemployed Jamaican baker in Birmingham in 1962. All, no doubt, in a day's – or in Swanwick's case, less than a week's – work as he successfully clambered the ladder to further success and official recognition of the highest order.

Swanwick's garish vision of a criminal underworld was as much a product of his own feverish imagination as, perhaps, of a wider societal apprehension of an increasingly visible 'other'. But was there even a sniff of validity in his notion of dangerous elements living on the fringes of a nether world? It probably played well enough with the good people of Birmingham fulfilling their civic duty that week, but was it fair and was it honest? Evidence suggests that it was not.

One thing we know for certain about Oswald Grey is that he had a gun in his possession at some point and, as would not have been the case for Graham Swanwick, such ownership would have been illegal. We can also be sure that Grey was not intending to use it for the purpose of exterminating a specially reared gamebird in flight. In Birmingham in 1962 as now, despite reporting that may lead us to believe otherwise, the use and possession of firearms for criminal purposes was rare. Its inhabitants, however, would not have been coy about the existence and use of such weaponry: it had been instrumental in building the city's wealth.

Even as a native of the city, it came as a surprise to me in my teenage years to discover that the company BSA made anything other than motorcycles. By that time, I had begun to appreciate just how coveted some of their products could be, and the fact that ownership of machines with glorious names like Bantam, Thunderbolt and Starfire could only lead to unimagined popularity, especially with girls. What must have been two or three years after Oswald Grey's death, I have a recollection of seeing the factory in Armoury Road, Small Heath – just under three miles from Lee Bank Road – and being mightily impressed by the three majestic towers, each bearing one of the initial letters. In what is a common, time-related disappointment for us all as we grow older, it was rather deflating to unearth a photograph of the squat, unprepossessing little blocks where production took place. By then, moreover, I knew the relevance of the acronym – Birmingham Small Arms. The company might have been making motorbikes in the 1960s, but its basic business had always been guns.

To be entirely accurate, although its origins were in the manufacture of arms, BSA had been, since its inception in 1861, the very model of industrial nimbleness, repurposing to suit markets and changing circumstances as it went along. When it was first granted a licence – and some healthy contracts – by the War Office, its principal purpose was to produce firearms, but the company never confined itself to this one activity. Over the years, it produced parts for bicycles and then knocked out components for the new-fangled motor car at the start of the twentieth century. A conglomeration of small manufacturers, it had started life in the city's Gun Quarter, just north of the hospital in Steelhouse Lane where Thomas Bates had breathed his last. At the start of the twentieth century, the city employed around 4,000 people in the gun industry. A plaque outside the current Bull pub, still standing in Price Street, proudly declares that the city was 'the foremost arms producer in the world'.

The Gun Quarter, like the neighbouring Jewellery Quarter, now celebrates its industrial, hard-scrabble past by embracing a gentrification that is content to glide over the use of its products in warfare and slaughter from Ireland to West Africa and beyond. Property developers – albeit in pre-pandemic times – promise that 'the Gun Quarter has as much, if not more, to offer, including the historical buildings, such as the listed pub The Bull's Head, with the same or more potential than the Jewellery Quarter'. They go on to claim that 'we will be mentioning the Gun Quarter and the Jewellery Quarter in the same breath when it comes to city living in the next 10 years'. By a cruel twist of fate, these prospective, prestigious dwellings will find themselves abutting those areas of the city where, in recent times, gun-related crime has been at its most prevalent.

For all of which, such crime remains mercifully rare in the UK. An authoritative Home Office Research Report of 2006 identified that 0.4% of serious crime was gun-related and that is a figure that has remained constant since. However, as the report points out, 'a small number of high-profile and shocking firearm homicides (raise) considerable public concerns about the problem of illegal firearms'. What the report, and the research behind it, also reveals is that such crime occurs with much greater proportional frequency among Black communities, an observation borne out by a later publication from the Centre for Crime and Justice in 2008. The authors collected data to demonstrate that 'Black communities, especially their younger members, appear disproportionately *victimised* by weapon-induced crime' (my emphases). Both publications draw a clear correspondence between the possession of guns and dance music, urban music and clubbing, but without equating these elements with matters of ethnicity.

What both reports also demonstrate is that the actual number of firearms in circulation is relatively small – to be measured in the low hundreds even in large cities – and that individual weapons are often trafficked from location to location for use in individual, specific episodes. In 2018, a BBC investigation by

Ashitha Nagesh followed the itinerary of 'Gun No. 6' from a crime in the Gun Quarter (in its dogged, pre-gentrified state) to eleven further crimes nationwide. This frequent transference of a weapon into different sets of hands has the strongest of echoes with the movements of the Walther 7.6 mm from its provenance in the home of Harold Bacchus in Varna Road – almost certainly not its original location – to its uncertain and unverified journey around Cannon Hill Road, Mary Street, Lozells and Lee Bank Road in May and June of 1962.

By a strange quirk of fate, it is entirely possible that there may have been just as many guns around in British society in 1962, although not necessarily in circulation, as there are in 2021. At the end of the Second World War, despite the efforts of the government, plenty of firearms found their way into the possession of British citizens, albeit that most of them probably remained as nothing more than decorative, decommissioned artefacts in cupboards, drawers and attics. Once hostilities had started, an advert appeared in newspapers in the USA in 1940, sponsored by the American Committee for the Defense (sic) of British Homes, the precursor of the National Rifle Association. This is, of course, the organisation whose representatives spring up with weary predictability after each US mass shooting to proclaim it all had nothing to do with making guns available to people who should never have been anywhere near them. British citizens, the advert proclaimed, had been 'stripped of their guns by their own government's policies' and so it was up to their American counterparts to rearm them by sending donations that would, in their turn, be shipped off to the Civilian Committee for the Protection of Homes. The headquarters of this body was located in the UK's own gun capital of Birmingham.

Much of this weaponry, from here and more official sources, found its way into the hands of the civil defence movement, the Home Guard – an organisation now irredeemably stamped into the consciousness of the British people via the situation comedy

Dad's Army. Not all of it was recovered when the war ended. These arms, along with others smuggled away from returning troop ships as souvenirs, were often a potential source of income to be gleaned from a criminal fraternity to whom they would always have been of interest. Guns, albeit not in huge numbers, were around and available to those who sought them out.

Swanwick's purpose was to depict a sub-group of society that wilfully rejected its mores, habits and expectations. Illegal gun ownership, and with it an obvious willingness to use such weapons for nefarious purposes, immediately put that stamp on such people. Along with this behaviour went insobriety and a general tendency towards intemperance. As far as this aspect of life was concerned, a new and disturbing menace seemed to be emerging in the 1960s and the 'other', and, in particular, the Black other, was the agent seen to be smuggling it in to disrupt propriety and order. Cannabis.

There is no dispute that cannabis was traditionally used in the Caribbean for recreational and therapeutic reasons. In Britain, prior to the 1950s, its use was not unknown but was largely considered to be the province of 'lascars' – a generic and slightly pejorative term for sailors and merchant seaman from the Indian subcontinent or, in looser usage, dark people from unknown lands hanging around ports. In his authoritative and entertaining book about the drug's consumption in Britain, *Cannabis Nation*, James H. Mills traces its importance in cultural, political and criminal terms in the eighty years from 1928. In a chapter whose title directly cites an official report of the time, *The prevalence of hashish smoking among the coloured men: migration communism and crime 1945-1962*, he reveals events and attitudes to post-war immigrants that has a familiar ring to modern ears.

Mills identifies a grubby tale of murder and deception in North London in 1952 as a turning point in attitudes towards a drug that, until that point, had scarcely made any impact on the collective consciousness. Both victim and culprit were Black.

The former, Joseph Aaku, was of Nigerian descent and the latter, Backary Manneh, originated from Gambia. They had much in common. Both had reached England as stowaways and both, as *de facto* British citizens, were then simply required to pay fines for their illegal mode of entry before becoming fully accredited nationals of their motherland. Both men had seen active service during the Second World War – Aaku in the army in Burma and Manneh in the Royal West Africa Frontier Force. And both men, it seemed, liked to smoke a joint or, to use the term current at the time, a reefer.

For all of the similarities in background, the lives they lived once on British soil could not have been more different. Joseph Aaku had managed to find solid, semi-skilled work as a carriage oiler at Euston station which paid him £8 a week. He had settled into a flat close to his work in Oakley Square, where he lived with his girlfriend, Teresa Maher, as man and wife – a status legitimised for them by her wearing of a gold ring. Conversely, Backary Manneh's life was one characterised by drifting, petty crime and the serial misfortune which is the hallmark of such an existence. The detail of the episode and Manneh's trial, examined forensically in Hill's book (he clearly had better fortune than me when searching for court records), reveal a British judiciary and press whose understandable ignorance about cannabis and its effects would raise smiles for the modern reader if the matter at stake had not been the lives and deaths of two men.

The bare bones of the case are that on 5 January 1952, there seems to be little doubt that Backary Manneh stabbed and killed Joseph Aaku in the latter's flat and then ran off with his watch. The initial police investigation concerned itself solely with the idea that robbery was the motive for the crime, but details emerged that held deep fascination during the trial that followed. A search of Aaku's premises had uncovered a blood-soaked packet of hemp. A witness at the trial then testified to the fact that he often saw both men in The Roebuck pub, where they were known to be 'hemp smokers'. Manneh was in possession of the drug when arrested. Teresa Maher conceded that she had witnessed Aaku smoking the drug on a few occasions, the effect of which was to 'make him rather happy, just as though he had had a few drinks'. The trial of Backary Manneh, and the general discourse that developed around it, embraced, with gleeful prurience, a lurid narrative of Black men driven wide-eyed and crazy by narcotic consumption.

In an attempt to suggest a case of diminished responsibility, the defence argued that Manneh, in his drug-induced haziness, could not have been fully responsible for his actions. The prosecution was having none of it. Calling on the significant expertise of Dr Donald Macintosh Johnson, the author of *Indian Hemp: A Social Menace*, they asked him to confirm his assertion that 'a few grains will send a person into a state of mania and violence'. Was he prepared to stand by his published observation that 'marijuana ...is closely linked with outbreaks of violence of a sudden and unexpected nature'? He most certainly was. Which must have rendered the jury, themselves unlikely to be much acquainted with the drug in the Britain of 1952, a touch confused when another medical man, Dr Robert Teare, was just as adamant that the drug's effects were somewhat more soporific. 'My readings have led me to believe,' he told the court, 'that ....it made ordinary things appear delightful, it made bad food taste good and it made boredom more bearable.' The standpoints of Doctors Johnson and Teare resurface still in the debate about the drug some seventy years on.

The efforts of the defence came to nothing and Manneh became another of Albert Pierrepoint's victims at Pentonville in May 1952. The reporting of his trial and his eventual demise provide a grim precursor for the fate of Oswald Grey, the coverage of whose crimes and death in his local paper are almost encyclopaedic by comparison. Four short lines in *The Western Mail* on 15 January 1952 under the headline 'Coloured man charged with murder' furnish the baldest of brief details. The *Daily Mirror* of the same day is only able to embellish these by informing us that Manneh had his arm in a sling and was wearing a black cloak. His next appearance in *The Mirror* is on 13 May under a much larger, bolder headline following his failed appeal: 'Primitive man lied in fear' we are told. Lord Justice Goddard was disinclined to exercise clemency for the poor brute whose victim, the paper informs us, 'had smoked himself into a frenzy'. One has to assume that the proceedings had not been closely followed by the defending counsel of Mahmood Hussein Mattan in Cardiff who, pretty well contemporaneously, offered the equally insulting, lame and ineffective plea that his client was a 'half child of nature; a semi-civilised savage'.

For one of the main pillars of the state, the police, this early correspondence between everything under the banner of cannabis – hemp, marijuana, reefers – and Black immigrants, set the tone for a volatile association that still plays out on the streets of Britain. By 1951, the number of drug-related offences, often arising from pre-planned raids of 'coloured' venues, underwent a slight increase. This was enough to prompt an over-nervous Home Office memo from Frank Thornton, the Head of the UK's Drugs Branch, who expressed the following fear:

Unless something can be done by the authorities concerned to stem the invasion of unemployed coloured men (mostly British subjects) from Africa and the British West Indies, we shall in this country, in a very short space of time, be faced with a serious hashish smoking problem....they are of little use in our labour market and.... they associate with lower class white girls, drink, peddle hashish cigarettes and generally present a problem to the police.

There had been 128 convictions for drug offences in 1951 in comparison with 86 the previous year and 70 for the years between 1944 and 1947. Although the increase in numbers is minimal, the die had been cast and the linkage between Black immigrants, cannabis, wild behaviour and crime was firmly established, if only in the influential imaginations of some in authority.

The forces of law and order may well have had an early inkling of the losing battle on which they were about to embark when it came to controlling the distribution and consumption of the drug. By 1961, a Metropolitan Police report could only glumly observe that 'there is still a demand by the coloured population of London for cannabis'. Even in pre-motorway days, dope aplenty must have found its way to Birmingham and beyond. However, the concerns of the authorities were no longer confined to the use of the drug in the communities of the new arrivals, as white kids enthusiastically began to latch on to it. In time, the association between the drug, emerging 'alternative' cultures and its significance as an emblem of defiance towards the fading, imperialist world and attitudes of post-war Britain, meant that its use spread far beyond the cramped dwellings of Oakley Square, Handsworth or Balsall Heath.

By the start of the 1960s, the forces of law and order had no hesitation in defining cannabis as a problem that was firmly rooted in the immigrant communities, but with potential to spread beyond these populations and thus constituting a worrying threat to wider society. By 1962, a Central Conference of Chief Constables was able to agree that 'there had been a very considerable increase in the misuse of this substance and in traffic in it' and although 'this increase is largely due to the increase of the coloured population in London', of equal, if not greater, concern was the fact that 'its use was spreading to white people, particularly young people'. According to James Mills, they needn't have been so agitated. Even with its gradual emergence as a white countercultural drug, evidence suggests that its use remained sporadic among white youth. 'Where it was consumed,' Mills writes, 'new users were more likely to have tried the drug through association with migrant groups than with radical politics and were as commonly workers or labourers as they were students or the offspring of the well-to-do.'

The authorities' anxieties about cannabis then, as now, seem hopelessly misplaced. They appear to have been more concerned about using the drug as an excuse to exercise prejudicial power over a despised minority group than any duty to maintain public order. Screeching headlines about the *Marihuana Menace* and *The Girl Who Tried Reefer Smoking* played along neatly with notions of exotic others bringing their dubious habits to our shores. But even though cannabis was a popular drug among some of West Indian origin, the stubbornly prevalent intoxicant of choice was plain old alcohol.

A search through the copious first-hand testimony from the Windrush Generation in Colin Grant's *Homecoming* reveals almost no mention of drug-taking as part of people's social lives. The blues parties referred to in Chapter 4, however, merit frequent comment as do the illicit drinking venues, shebeens, that were clearly part of the same scene. One of Grant's interviewees, Owen Townsend, recalls the prevalence of such institutions:

You had blues parties...on top of that you you've got the shebeens. A blues party was like an occasional party, so Friday night, Saturday night. The shebeen was seven days a week, more or less twenty-four/seven. They weren't licensed, they were called illegal, but only in the sense that the drinks were sold and the taxman wasn't getting a cut; but they were the hub of the community, especially for young people like myself who were not long come from Jamaica.

For another new arrival, Sonia Saunders, younger than Townsend, the parties were less exciting affairs. She recalls being 'dragged along' to the events that were usually 'in a front room packed with people laughing their heads off' with 'gold teeth on full display ... and the smells of cigarette smoke, alcohol and curry goat and rice on the stove'. For adults, however, they offered something even Graham Swanwick, eager to create a grimy world of feckless rascals, would have fully understood: jolly company, good food and, importantly, heady liquor.

Appreciation of these delights was built into the training of his profession of choice. What is more, they were, and remain, compulsory. In March 2019, the Law Society issued a memorandum to its members reminding them that the centuries' old tradition of mandatory 'dining sessions' were to continue after the Bar Standards Board said it recognised the vital role played by such meetings. No record exists of the fare on offer at the Inns of Court in Swanwick's time, but his current counterparts can enjoy lunch in 'our stunning Elizabethan Hall' on weekdays for £32.50 per head, where, according to one recent restaurant critic 'one could imagine oneself in someone's Dordogne cottage, kitted out cheaply and eclectically so as to discourage winter burglaries or perhaps in the English house of a kindred soul who would not dream of possessing a matching dinner service'. For a man who enjoyed his country pursuits, it must have felt like home from home for Graham Swanwick. He was probably unable – or disinclined – to make the leap of imagination that would have let him appreciate any correspondence between the way he and his set and those around Oswald Grey took their pleasures. Far better, for his professional purpose, to allow the dark fantasy of a shady underworld to prevail.

Swanwick married twice and nothing exists to suggest that his private life was anything other than entirely proper. He may have been as appalled as any of his contemporaries by the perception bedevilling those who revel in comfortable decency, that moral disorder creeps ever closer to threaten 'our' way of life. That Oswald Grey spent much of his time in Balsall Heath and, most particularly, the area around Varna Road, could only have helped him as he attempted to convince a jury, aware, no doubt, of the reputation of the area, that the accused was more than comfortable slinking around such streets of shame. Strangely, it is accounts from two rather different immigrants that illuminate something of the area which, to reiterate, I experienced almost daily, blithely unaware of either its notoriety or the turpitude that prompted it.

Kate Paul was born in Jerusalem in 1940 and by the early 1960s was working as a teacher in Birmingham. Cheap lodgings were to be had in Balsall Heath, in a street where, in her own words, 'to be white is exceptional'. She describes a place 'of brothels and men hanging about on street corners' coexisting with 'a few old women (who) walk slowly up the street carrying shopping bags'. Paul bemoans the suspicion and fear she sees around her, but her contempt is reserved for the men in cars who 'kerb crawl and raise their fingers, leaning forward, eager, their faces drawn with lust'. 'I hate these,' she rails, 'not the streetwalkers.' Police visits are perfunctory in a neighbourhood of slamming doors, shrill voices and vulgar insults.

Among it all, gentleness and decency persist. She talks of an 'amazingly kind' old couple upstairs and her journal is enlivened by her persistent political idealism and activism. In this, there are echoes of the astonishing work of American photographer, Janet Mendelsohn, whose portfolio of photographic work of Varna Road is startlingly evocative. A graduate of Radcliffe College, Harvard, her work depicts the Road some five years after Grey's execution, but the images present ocular proof that little could have changed to improve the neighbourhood's shabbiness. Nonetheless, the work is infused with a tenderness and humanity that convey, in the words of those who collated her photographs, 'a self-confidence amongst the immigrant population and a growing permanence embodied in Balsall Heath's built environment'. Such qualities, of course, do not fit a narrative of lives that readily embrace feckless depravity.

That there were parts of the city where prostitution was common, where drunken fights took place – sometimes over imagined insults, fanned and intensified by alcohol – and which occurred in areas which any half-sensible adult would know to avoid, especially after dark, is scarcely worthy of intelligent attention. That such areas were usually characterised by poverty and precarious ways of living and, inevitably, by new waves of immigrants who, in their turn, were often single, unattached young men, is equally unremarkable. However, airbrushing out those parts of such communities typified by upright, considerate citizens, who worked hard to better themselves, their families and their neighbourhood, proved, unsurprisingly, to be too convenient a choice to make for a man who was treading his own predetermined path from public school, to Oxford to the High Court and on to knighthood. Such gilded highways were inaccessible for all but the most privileged who had come from Jamaica and other Caribbean locations.

For the majority who arrived in the main wave of 1950s immigration, the strong likelihood was that their education would have finished at primary level, especially if they came from rural areas. Access to secondary school was rare and where it did exist, it mirrored and mimicked a version of the English grammar school, communicating an idealised and largely misleading view of life in the mother country. Bert Williams, later awarded the MBE for his voluntary service to Black and ethnic minority people, came to Britain in 1960 and recalls schooldays in Jamaica where 'our exam paper, our 'O' Levels, were sent from and had to come back to England to be marked'. The curriculum was an obvious reflection of this: history 'was about Churchill and the economy was about Bristol iron works and Sheffield steel'. Nonetheless, this shot at education furnished him with a significant head start over most immigrants of the time.

The possibility of self-improvement was proffered in the scattered and sporadic provision of evening classes for adults, or 'night school', but opportunities to avail themselves of this was not realistically open to many – especially after long, physically demanding days at work, followed, particularly for women, by domestic chores and obligations. The National Institute of Continuing Adult Education had been established in 1921 with the remit to widen this sort of service, but by 1945, the range of services on offer was diminishing. Nevertheless, night school provided a lifeline that was eagerly grabbed by many. Another MBE, DJ Norman Jay, born in Notting Hill to parents who had arrived from Grenada, recalls how his father became a 'grade one civil engineer on London Transport, having worked his way up from going to night school and getting all his certificates'. MP David Lammy tells of how his Guyanese mother would go twice a week to improve her typing speeds, until she 'eventually graduated with the City and Guilds certificate that hung proudly on our living room wall throughout my childhood'. She retired from a senior position in Haringey council thirty years later. Such successes were proof positive to many immigrants that education was, indeed, the key to a better life in their new home.

For too many, however, their experience of the formal education of their children was a dispiriting business. Schools were ill-equipped and poorly prepared when it came to dealing with children who very often had been in receipt of the most rudimentary education and who had come to join their parents. If there was a case to say that this lack of preparation was excusable, what was less pardonable was the racism, both overt and implicit, suffered by such children from many teachers who hobbled them with the crippling burden of low expectation. To compound matters, the crude, and now thoroughly discredited, measure of Intelligence Quotient (IQ) tests was used as a major determinant of a child's 'ability'. Questions relating to tennis courts and cinema prices immediately disadvantaged children unfamiliar with entities that were culturally specific and beyond their childhood experience. Poor performance in the tests and the distracted and disengaged behaviour of many young people – who were gradually understanding their disenfranchisement from a system that didn't want them – were clear signs of educational 'subnormality'.

In 2021, the film company Rogan Productions produced the TV documentary *Subnormal: A British Scandal*. Included in the varied testimony are contributions from two Black Brummies, Maisie Barrett and Anne Marie Simpson, both of whom had fallen victim to the precipitate rush to place children of Caribbean origin outside the mainstream of the education system.

In common with many other children in the mid-1960s, Anne Marie had been left behind in Jamaica while her parents established themselves in Birmingham. Her education on the island was fragmented and rudimentary. When she left her homeland at nine years old, she found herself in a 'cold, damp' country, her 'fairy tale shattered' and ending up with a mother who was indifferent to her newly arrived offspring. 'I was lost, lonely and disappointed ... and who was in my corner?' Certainly not the teachers who failed to understand that her disruptive and aggressive behaviour – 'I was always getting into fights' – stemmed from her inability to read and write. Her persistence and determination ensured that she eventually built a professional career for herself, working as a social worker with children with special educational needs. Her success came despite, not because of, a system that was stacked against her.

Maisie Barrett was also labelled 'backward' by a school that, in common with most at the time, was unable to recognise dyslexia. Birmingham-born of Caribbean parents, she tells of how she endured having her ears pulled for not paying attention in classes where she was stultified by boredom brought on by her inability to follow what was happening. Even in the supposedly special setting of her new school, she encountered prejudicial treatment: 'I just thought it was normal for white children to get more support than us, the Black children.' A stroke of luck ended with her dyslexia being diagnosed and addressed. In her later years, she has embarked on a lifetime of diverse study, culminating in a degree in Caribbean Studies and Creative Writing. Nonetheless, she admits to finding it difficult to settle into patterns of regular employment and considers her early disadvantage to have played out to the detriment of her own wellbeing and that of her family.

It took until the start of the decade following Oswald Grey's death for this systemic malaise to be addressed. Arriving in Britain from Grenada in 1966, Bernard Coard set off for the University of Sussex to begin his degree in political economy. In the years that followed, as he pursued his academic career, he earned money working as a teacher in two schools for the Educationally Subnormal (ESN) in East London. As with much we encounter from a mere sixty years ago, the language – and the attitudes revealed by that language – is stark and shocking to modern ears. Quite what a bewildered young person, for whom school had already been something of a mysterious trial, would have made of being labelled 'subnormal', doesn't tax the imagination too greatly. Coard was appalled by what he experienced and decided to do something about it.

Several issues horrified him. First was the disproportionate number of children of Caribbean heritage, born both in the UK or overseas, in such schools. Then there were the low expectations of poorly trained – and just as poorly paid – teachers. Beyond that, there was a curriculum unsuitable in just about every way for children who would almost certainly be condemned to a cycle of deprivation unless education offered some sort of potential escape route. Reflecting on his time in ESN schools, Coard, writing in 2004 after an extraordinary life to which we will return, recalls that 'in the education system as a whole, I discovered that the system was using the ESN schools as a convenient dumping ground for Black children who were anything but 'educationally subnormal'.' It prompted him to write a short but enormously influential book in 1971, with an important but not particularly pithy title: *How the West*

Indian Child is Made Educationally Subnormal in the British School System: The Scandal of the Black Child in Schools in Britain. The formulation of the title is significant. Coard was arguing against a strain of thought that clung enthusiastically to the false notion that something inherent in children rendered them inferior. By emphasising the idea that the child was *made* subnormal by a deficient system, Coard was taking aim at the entrenched pedagogic and political values and practices of the time.

Significantly, however, it was not the constituency of the great and the good at whom Coard was aiming his writing.

I took a critical decision. I would address the book explicitly to Black parents. Not to teachers, not to the education and political authorities, not to the public at large; exclusively to Black parents. I wanted to get them conscious of the problems, and organised to deal with them. I wanted them to feel personally spoken to; to recognize that this was a problem that they had to get up and tackle; not rely on any others to do on their behalf.

Within months of publication, thousands of Black parent groups were established and Coard estimates that some 150 supplementary schools were established as parents worked to compensate for the deficit that had plagued their children's schooling. He talks of addressing as many as three evening meetings a week as he, and those around him, toiled tirelessly to ensure that the issue remained alive and important. These efforts paid dividends: by the time I started my own teacher training in 1975, Coard's book had become central reading for those about to embark on careers in secondary schools. By then, Coard had returned to Grenada and was on the road to a career in politics that saw him hold the office of Prime Minister for three days in 1983, before being sentenced to death, commuted to life imprisonment, for alleged involvement in the murder of the previous incumbent, Maurice Bishop. He was released in 2009.

Even during his imprisonment, Coard's interest in the topic that had so enflamed him in 1971 had not waned. In his article for the *Guardian* in 2004, he expressed his anger at the established, persistent trend of the exclusion of Black children from British schools. These suspensions, he argued, 'of disproportionately Black kids – from school because of misbehaviour (of various sorts and gravity) does not solve society's – or these youths' – problems'. It 'postpones, while making worse, the day of society's reckoning for having failed to educate and cherish these youths when they were younger'. He will be dismayed, no doubt, by the figures seventeen years on which show that Black children are three times more likely to be suspended or excluded than their white counterparts.

Yet Coard's writing and, more particularly, the agency among Black parents that it stimulated, provides a compelling antidote to Graham Swanwick's community of other people who hovered around the fringes of upright society and who he was more than content to characterise as living lives beyond the boundaries of respectability. For Swanwick, whose job it was to condemn Grey, notions of self-improvement and the possibilities of what we now call social mobility ran counter to a narrative of unreliable people wandering their way through feckless, directionless lives.

There is no recorded comment from the twelve citizens who sat in judgement on Oswald Grey. They were part of a society as yet unused to large numbers of people from elsewhere living among them. It is impossible to believe that they could have been immune to a prevailingly negative discourse about those who had come to their city. What's more, in a society still characterised by great deference to those in positions of recognised authority, to have heard confirmation of some of their worst suspicions from the bewigged and supremely confident man of law would have been highly persuasive. Their brief period of deliberation – less than an hour – is a further suggestion that this would have been the case. Swanwick would have made an experienced professional's assessment about the prejudices and partialities that those who would decide Grey's fate would bring to the courtroom. Despite the likely differences in lifestyle and background between himself and those on jury service for that brief week, persuading them that Oswald Grey was not like us would have gone a long way to convincing him that this was another successful day's work as he retired smugly to his chambers.

Chapter 8

November 1962. Castro and Marilyn hit the headlines. A Birmingham execution goes unnoticed.

The impending fall of civilisation can cast a pall over childhood. In the weeks between Oswald Grey's trial and execution, I was burdened by images of machines, or something or other, screeching in the skies above me and then obliterating everything below them in a blinding flash. My mother, like so many women of her generation and experience, seemed her usual war-hardened and stoic self, but there was no doubting my sisters' anxiety – and there was no evading the unease that they managed to transfer to me. The Russians, whose leader was grumpy looking old Kruschev, were going to set off some nuclear bombs and the person on whom we were pinning our faith to stop him was handsome, dependable John F Kennedy. But things didn't seem to be looking good.

I wouldn't want the reader to run away with the idea that I was a nine-year-old with some kind of prematurely savant view of geopolitics. I liked cricket, football and reading and I am most certainly not one of that breed of people – and I come across plenty – who has ascribed to a perfectly normal rough-and-tumble post-war upbringing, some superimposed, and usually self-centred, notion of deprivation or general want. But while, for the most part, I trundled through the movie of my life with me as the only worthwhile actor of note, stuff outside my little orbit sometimes found a way into swirling, randomised childhood consciousness. My older sisters often provided the conduits for these.

I expect the modern era might have found some way of making an engaging, light-hearted documentary out of discussions of the

Cuban missile crisis in the playground of a Birmingham primary school. The internet reveals no such recordings, although some fifty years after the event, America's National Public Radio Network – still resolutely attracting an audience of some 28 million people a week in the era of Wild-West news – sought the recollections of two Americans of Cuban heritage. One of these was Marta Darby, now a food writer, whose memories cast light on events taking place against a recent, wartime past that provoked a hauntingly unpleasant echo for her friends and family. She talks of how:

> *There was a group of Cuban kids that I went to school with. We lived in Miami and our school had mostly Jewish kids and Cuban kids. And we talked about this. I do remember talking about this amongst ourselves. And I think at the time we were afraid that maybe something would happen to us much like the Japanese internment camps during World War II. And there were whispers of that. Maybe they'll take us away and hide us somewhere. And that was a little bit scary.*

In the haphazard way that memory works, my own anxious recall sees me, on a Sunday morning after cheder (Jewish school), walking across Calthorpe Park with a small gang of chums to the 48 bus stop on Edward Street, just around the corner from Mary Street, where Oswald Grey claimed he had spent the afternoon of 2 June 1962 in Pious's café. Our agreed position on the crisis was clear: there were two possibilities. The first was by far the least desirable. If the Russians, who were stupid and, see above, governed by a fat old man, decided to start a war, nuclear bombs would start whizzing across the world between America and Russia. Because we were friends with America, Russia would send some bombs to us as well. These bombs would be dreadful but, mercifully, would finish you off very quickly because you'd burn up to dust if you were near them. Just like the people in Japan where they'd had a nuclear bomb. You'd just end up as a black shadow on the ground. We'd seen pictures. Notwithstanding the mitigating effects of this almost painless end, I do remember all of us admitting to being very scared.

The second potential outcome – and, to be honest, the one we all kind of knew would come to pass – was that the Russians would chicken out because America's weapons would obviously be better than theirs. An indisputable fact of life was that everything in America was bigger, better and shinier. We had to concede that a flaw in this plan was that the Russian leaders didn't care about their people and so would gladly sacrifice them in the quest to get one over on America and handsome John Kennedy – our mothers all loved him – and, besides, under communism, where everyone had to pretend they were equal or they'd be killed off, people just did as they were told anyway because they were deliberately kept in darkness and ignorance. So even though there was an outside chance that Kruschev would just charge on regardless, he'd be sure to see sense in the end, wouldn't he?

The most cursory of searches for serious, academic literature in books and articles about the Cuban missile crisis reveals an initial 113,000 entries. I strongly suspect that none of the authors or contributors was ever trudging across a park in Balsall Heath in 1962 and that the nuances of the brinkmanship taking place in October of that year would have been far beyond the ken of that little group. However, on the evening of 20 November 1962, a few hours after Harry Allen had completed his grisly task in Winson Green Prison, President John F Kennedy, satisfied that all Russian weaponry had been dismantled or shipped out of Cuba, lifted the naval blockade of that island. If the crisis had demonstrated that neither power was, thank goodness, prepared to risk the mutually assured destruction that would be inflicted by the use of nuclear weapons, there ensued a quarter of a century when both sides, and their allies, felt compelled to start up the arms race that would commandeer huge swathes of their national economies for decades to come.

As I say, much of my connection with this wider world came from what I picked up from my sisters. In 1961, my elder sibling, some ten years my senior, had developed an interest that was either reflective of something personal or may have been related to her studies; she had just started training to be a primary school teacher. On 11 April 1961, the trial of Adolph Eichmann, one of Hitler's most senior henchmen, who had brought his dull, organisational skills to the enterprise of mass human slaughter, began in Jerusalem. He had been captured the year before by members of Israel's secret service, Mossad, in Argentina. In her forensically detailed account of his trial and the moral and ethical issues it raised, Hannah Arendt's *Eichmann in Jerusalem*, chose to subtitle the work *A Report on the Banality of Evil*. She was referring not only to the careful, sometimes plodding legal processes that were being enacted in Jerusalem, but also to the spectacle of someone who had been an unexceptional school student and a relatively successful salesman, now making his mark on the world through careful, administrative actions that insulted humanity. From the start of his trial, my sister put together her collection of press cuttings to which I paid passing attention, yet obviously absorbing something of their significance along the way.

Eichmann's trial lasted 56 days until 14 August 1961 when it was adjourned for various deliberations. On 12 December, guilty verdicts were announced and three days later, he was condemned to hang. His principal appeals took place between 22 and 29 March in 1962, none of which succeeded in overturning either the verdict or the sentence. Eichmann's final appeal for clemency, in a four-page handwritten letter, was first considered by Israel's President Yitzhak Ben-Zvi on 29 May and on the advice of Prime Minister Ben-Gurion and his Cabinet, was, in its turn, rejected. Eichmann was informed of this at 8.00 p.m.

on 31 May and thereafter, matters advanced apace. With no three-Sunday rule or anything like it in place, his execution was scheduled for midnight on 31 May.

There is some dispute as to exactly when the execution took place. Hannah Arendt is clear that it was shortly before midnight, but William L Hull, who was the chaplain appointed to provide spiritual counsel to Eichmann, describes it, in his book *The Struggle for a Soul,* as taking place a few minutes after, on 1 June – the day before Thomas Bates decided not to go to watch the cricket at Edgbaston.

Other than that, once the spectre of the blood-stained man had slunk back into the shadows – albeit that I'd still cast the occasional wary glance at a number 8 – little else from the outside world pierced the introspective armour of childhood. In September I moved from Mrs Kaye's class to Mrs Bloom's and before the leaves had turned had already received a few pre-emptive, if perfunctory, canings, really just *pour encourager les autres*. By then, the Russians were unloading nuclear missiles in the Cuban port of Mariel, and England's cricketers had completed the wearisome task of defeating their mismatched Pakistani opponents. Unnoticed, it seems, by any but the closest few, Oswald Grey languished in Winson Green Prison awaiting his trial. For my nine-year-old self, one other external event wriggled its way in.

On 5 August 1962, the death of Marilyn Monroe was announced. I knew she was a film star, very famous and very pretty. I honestly don't think I knew the word 'sexy' at the time, but however imperfectly formed my thoughts, or however deficient the language then at my disposal, there were definite stirrings when I saw pictures of her. The news reached me during a family visit to an aunt's house and once the conversations started, I knew, as a matter of indisputable fact, that there was something saucy afoot. There was an immediate and obvious indication.

My mother, her sisters and brothers-in-law were all born and bred in Birmingham and all but one still lived there. The only sister to make a break and who was not there that day had become a GI bride. She lived in impossibly glamorous New York – as it turned out, in a modest apartment block in the Bronx. One of the many things, however, that they had all clung onto from their heritage was their knowledge of Yiddish. It's a language whose origins and nature are often misunderstood. The Oxford English Dictionary blandly defines it as being 'a German dialect with words from Hebrew and several modern languages'. A definition that comes a little closer to capturing its essence as an attitude to life as much as mere means of communication is Michael Wex's observation in *Born to Kvetch* that it 'is a language that likes to argue with everyone about everything – and to do so all the time, even when it's pretending not to'. But there was one truth that us second-generation lot knew only too well: when the grown-ups chose to go into Yiddish, you knew that was where the good stuff – the scandals, the rudeness, the naughtiness – was being dealt with. And they were using it that day to mull over the death of Marilyn.

It seems they had plenty to keep them entertained. Monroe appeared to have committed suicide; her deathbed, as far as we could glean from the adults' conversation, had been scattered with pills and empty bottles. And then, a morsel so delicious, smuggled out to us by an older cousin, that it had us all children spluttering with giggles and bedevilled by racing imaginations. Marilyn had been found IN THE NUDE! The truth of this lasciviousness was confirmed by reports in the next day's *Daily Mirror*. Its fearless newsmen (it would be fair to attribute gender specificity here) informed us that 'the star who walked with a wiggle' had been discovered 'naked – as she always slept – and covered only by a sheet and a blanket'. What an astonishing place America must be and what extraordinary goings-on must there have been in the life of these glorious film stars. My aunts, of course, were less entranced. Us kids knew two frequently used Yiddish words for non-Jewish women. One was *shikseh* – generic in its meaning it was used for a young woman who simply wasn't of the faith, but almost onomatopoeic in the contemptuous way it was often spat out. The other was *kurveh*, which we didn't quite get as kids, but serves as a vulgar portmanteau term for a promiscuous woman. Poor old wiggly, naked Marilyn seemed to qualify on all counts.

And that was just about the world beyond Institute, St Luke's and Speedwell Roads for a fairly alert nine-year-old during the months that Oswald Grey waited to be tried, was convicted, lost his appeal and, eventually, his life. On the day of Marilyn Monroe's death, Nelson Mandela was arrested in the town of Howick in KwaZulu-Natal Province. The *Mirror* was one of the few papers to deem the capture of 'The Black Pimpernel' – a 'burly, dynamic ex-lawyer and boxer' and the 'most wanted man' on the list of apartheid supporting Prime Minister, Hendrik Verwoerd. For Mandela, it was the first day of a captivity that would last for 27 years. That he would eventually emerge as a genuinely iconic figure for Black activists around the globe would have been a prediction that could not possibly have figured in the narrow public – and global – political imagination of 1962. He disappeared, albeit temporarily, into quiet obscurity.

By contrast, lustrous John Kennedy was killed almost exactly a year after he had seen off Kruschev and Fidel Castro. The manner of his death and his legacy, both real and imagined, became inscribed forever in our collective consciousness and the more salacious end of the news market has busied itself since with idle speculation about the possibility of his night of secret passion with Monroe in March 1962. To suggest that nothing became Kennedy's life like the leaving of it might be too brusque and harsh a judgement. Unlike many who have held his office, the general wave of sympathy, accompanied by nostalgic folklore of our memories of our whereabouts at the time of his death, has meant that aspects of his private life and public decisions have benefited from relatively light-touch scrutiny. It is churlish, however, to deny that in a glum, monochrome sort of world, stubbornly clinging to the tail-end of wartime austerity, he represented anything other than a figure of hope and promise for many.

JFK and Marilyn. Cuba and Castro with his beard and cigar. Russia with fat old Kruschev terrifying his cowed people. Glamorous America and golden-flecked South Africa. Lands and people that existed only through the medium of news footage that mixed authority with a haughty condescension toward its audience. Holidays were at the seaside where you went into the sea to turn blue and be weighed down by swimming costumes made of super-absorbent cheap wool. Our end-of-term outing was to Drayton Manor Park in Tamworth, a creaking shadow of its current manifestation but a wonderland, nonetheless. We ventured little beyond our own back yards.

Jamaica only existed as a notion on a globe. In the decades that followed, many of us revelled in the talent of the sporting and musical stars who came from the island. In turn, this began to enhance our slim knowledge and appreciation of its culture, politics, music and food. But in 1962, we were ignorant. The minor leap of the imagination required to understand what it might have meant to board a ship, leaving one way of life to venture to another, was beyond most, including families like my own who were immigrants themselves. One reason – and it is only one – is obvious: with no experience of everyday life in different places, reference points were rare and any empathy that might have been generated, rarer still. Underpinning all of this was a prevailing deficit model: quite simply, other people were not as good as 'us'. Some were to be applauded for their aspirations – for 'integrating' – and there were aspects of custom and conduct that were endearingly close to our own, but, at base, they remained alien and their presence disconcerting.

November 1962. Castro and Marilyn hit the headlines.

And so it was that on a chilly, drizzly day at the end of November in 1962, the execution of an 'unemployed Jamaican baker' in Winson Green Prison, Birmingham, made no impact on the world whatsoever. By way of further example, here is a final, telling illustration of this anonymity.

I spend a diverting hour or so trawling internet sites of varying provenance and reliability, looking at prominent or important deaths in 1962. Almost all include clickbait alluding to Marilyn Monroe or Eichmann; there are literary figures – Vita Sackville-West, Hermann Hesse; eminent public people – Queen Wilhelmina and Eleanor Roosevelt; Nobel Prize winners – Niels Bohr; movie stars – Charles Laughton. Depending on their individual emphases, some sites include more politicians, sportspeople or entertainers, but, apart from Eichmann, no criminals – with one exception. Scroll down to early April 1962 and, from time to time, the name of James Hanratty pops up. He is deemed worthy of mention; he has made his mark on history. He will make the occasional appearance in a pub quiz. He has been remembered.

Chapter 9

Records lost in transit.
The creation of non-people.

You must take your passport with you as this is to prove you are a British Citizen.
From *Going to Britain*, a 1959 BBC booklet advising potential emigrants.

This is a book about a boy whose life has been forgotten. Indifferent officialdom, careless record-keeping and wanton racism have colluded in maintaining this shameful invisibility. Clumsy bureaucracy played its part in concealing him.

Those coming to Britain from the Caribbean were, of course, merely exercising the same right as someone moving from Newcastle to London when it came to choosing where to sell their labour. A British passport was all they needed. Sometimes even that was surplus to requirements as the stories of the easy accreditation of stowaways Backary Manneh and Joseph Aaku in Chapter 7 attest. The only paperwork required as newcomers stepped off boat or plane was this precious blue document and, if arriving by sea, a landing card. These will feature again shortly.

The booklet, *Going to Britain*, easily available online, is an unintentionally hilarious piece of work. The list of contents ascribes authorship to the different chapters, a couple of which were penned by Trinidadian author, Samuel Selvon. In 1956, Selvon's seminal work, *Lonely Londoners*, had charted the lives of several Caribbean newcomers. It is a work notable not just for its insight and empathy, but also for being written in a form of creolized English, an extraordinary literary development that seems to have gone largely unacknowledged. Other chapters have less notable provenance, and some are simply labelled as being the work of an anonymous 'West Indian Doctor'.

Newcomers are advised to maintain a degree of decorum in the lodging houses where they will probably take up initial residence. English people, the publication advises, 'are so quiet, you hardly know they are there – they are like that, they don't like noise or shouting'. There is advice about rent books, train fares and joining a trade union as soon you start work, although what local TGWU secretary Harry Green would have made of that (see Chapter 4 for his protectionist outlook) is a matter for conjecture. Sit with your workmates at breaktimes, clean the lavatory properly and never jump a queue.

Published in 1959, *Going to Britain* is an oddly ambivalent piece of work. The booklet is a sitting duck for gentle mockery from sixty years on but it is well-intentioned, comprehensive, practical and helpfully unsentimental about the 'mother country'. There are messages about preparing yourself for prejudicial attitudes, problems getting work and, without naming it as such, racism. Its foreword, written by Sir Grantley Adams, Prime Minister of the West Indies, captures this ambivalence. He doesn't quite say to the reader that he would sooner they didn't go rather than stay to build their own country, but he's not far off doing so. The information that follows, he explains, is provided neither to 'dissuade or persuade you'. Adams goes on to insist that 'It is very far from my mind to increase the flow of West Indians leaving these islands of ours' and that his government is 'doing everything in our powers to improve the living standards of our people'. Within the next few pages, the prospective traveller is warned that 'jobs are getting scarcer and scarcer' with 'people having been here for eight month who have not worked yet.' And it will be cold:

It is colder than anything you have ever felt. In the winter all the water outside freezes, that is it turns to ice. Everybody shivering though protected with warm sweaters, leather gloves, woollen coats and thick-soled shoes. Are you prepared for this cold climate with its icy winds, its sleet, its snow?

There follow any number of exhortations to try to fit in, not be a nuisance, take the first job you're offered and not to use the new National Health Service more often than is absolutely necessary.

Nowhere is this message about keeping a low-profile starker than when it comes to those areas which could provide some relief from the challenges which the booklet outlines – church, cricket and music parties.

When it comes to churchgoing, there is a strong echo of Bishop Joe Aldred's observation that engaging with other worshippers is no guarantee of any truly Christian spirit on their part. 'You may find friends there', the text suggests, 'but if you don't, you can get there a truer picture of what you're really up against'. On the cricket field, too, there are unsubtle, if comedic, warnings about how you may be both welcomed yet viewed suspiciously. You may well be invited to join your local cricket team, but if you do, always cheerfully accept the umpire's decision; after all, 'he may be the Village Squire'. And if you should invite others to your room for a West Indian style party, you must warn your 'merry guests not to stomp up and down the stairs if they are going to use the toilet' and ensure that you do not 'play your radio or radiogram at full volume, as if you were advertising the party'. In a more disturbing section, the booklet gives a measured warning about the perils of looking for entertainment beyond these domestic knees-ups. 'Dance halls in England', it warns, 'are the places to have fun and enjoy yourself (but) they are the places you are most likely to get into trouble if you don't behave yourself'.

We have no idea whether Felix Grey or his son read *Going to Britain* prior to their arrival. What is more, we are only able to make educated guesses as to when they arrived from Jamaica, whether they did so together and, in the case of Felix, what happened to him after his son's execution. An episode from the very recent past sheds some light on the bureaucratic sloppiness that makes the tracing of their movements such a frustrating business.

In April 2018, it came to light, through the actions of a whistle-blower, that the Home Office had ordered the destruction of thousands of disembarkation cards from immigrants from the Caribbean in the 1950s and 60s. The documents were housed in the government's Whitgift Centre in Croydon which closed in 2010. When staff were deployed to different locations, the Home Secretary at the time, Theresa May, ordered the destruction of the cards. Officials warned that this was a bad idea and that, as clumsy and cumbersome as this means or record-keeping may have been, the documentation contained vital evidence when it came to resolving individual cases pertaining to migration status, access to services and even the right to remain in the country. According to the informant, if, for example, the Passport Office made an inquiry about an individual, 'people would just say, "I'll have a look in the basement"' and the information would become available.

Such requests, although relatively infrequent, were thus dealt with no fuss other than a dusty tramp into the lower reaches of a government tower block. Once the cards had been destroyed, however, the only response staff were able to furnish, either to organisations or individuals, was that, regrettably, no records were available. All of which might just have been manageable, had it not been for a disastrously alarming political intervention announced by Theresa May in an interview for the *Daily Telegraph* in May 2012.

Running scared of the growing popularity Nigel Farage's anti-immigration UKIP party, as well as playing to that section of the Tory gallery perennially happy to lap up red-meat racism, May chose the moment to play with this particularly volatile political fire herself. 'The aim is to create here in Britain a really hostile environment for illegal migration,' she told the paper and in doing so, coined a phrase that both lodged in popular consciousness and which has stained her political career since.

In the weeks following her announcement, vans carrying advertising boards toured areas of the country where significant numbers of people with migrant heritage lived. If it wasn't quite the 'Wogs Go Home' or 'Keep Britain White' of bygone graffitied slogans, it wasn't far off. 'In the UK illegally?' snarled the large yellow and black lettering of the hazard warning. Beneath the question was the blunt order to 'go home or face arrest' along with a text number to help you avoid such detention and, no doubt, to book your passage to wherever that precarious location may have been. Leaflets in eighty languages were distributed in shops and community locations. Landlords were charged with checking the migrant status of potential tenants. Farage's ludicrous claims – Romanian crime waves, the flooding of the housing market with Greek money, the disappearance of spoken English on commuter trains – were left unchallenged by a government content to allow the association of 'others' with illegality and criminality to take hold.

The hostile environment and the negligent bureaucracy that followed, ruined lives. In a report published in December 2018, the National Audit Office (NAO) noted that many who had come to Britain from the Caribbean in the 1950s and 60s 'were never given documents and the Home Office kept no records'. As a consequence, the NAO reached the damning conclusion that as a result of this error, for the 'people who had been made vulnerable because of a lack of documentation' the government had 'failed to protect their rights to live, work and access services in the UK and many have suffered distress and material loss as a result'. To make matters worse, the report wearily observed, 'this was both predictable and forewarned.'

Abundant testimony came to light from those so affected. In March 2020, the *Guardian* newspaper produced a catalogue of dismay, sketching the lives of 50 such people who had fallen foul of this unspeakable failure of government officialdom. It reported on the deaths of a number of individuals whose health had been unable to withstand the distress they had encountered. There were Jamaicans aplenty among the dead and the living. Those who survived recounted woeful experiences.

Paulette Wilson, who had arrived in 1968 and had worked as a cook at the House of Commons, was informed that she was an illegal immigrant, prevented from working and sent to a detention centre at Yarl's Wood in Bedfordshire and from there to Heathrow for deportation. Only the intervention of her MP, Emma Reynolds, prevented her from being forced onto a plane. Valerie Baker left Jamaica in 1955 and worked all her life until a back problem forced her to retire. In 2017, the Home Office informed her that she had no legal basis to remain in the UK and ordered her to repay over £33 thousand in disability benefits. Her countryman, Winston Robinson, was sacked from his job as an ambulanceman because he had no passport – he had arrived when he was nine. Informed that he 'should take steps to leave the UK immediately' he was also told that he was ineligible for benefit payments and became homeless when he was unable to pay his rent.

As appalling as they may be, these bare bones from the scores of tales of people displaced within their own country, or summarily dismissed from their means of making a living, only tell a partial story. Their testimonies are littered with telling words and phrases. There is talk of betrayal and injustice. Lifelong taxpayers and those who had served in both the military and civil services express fury and bewilderment at their treatment. Those stranded in the places of their birth, be it after the birthday treat paid for by children or the funeral of a relative, express dismay at the way they have been both disregarded and dehumanised: 'we were invited here and then thrown away again like rubbish,' says Tony Perry who had served in the navy and then as a social worker in Haringey. The Home Office had, very swiftly, ditched the term 'hostile' in favour of creating a 'compliant environment' but this was a linguistic nicety lost on those whose only mistake was not to be in possession of a valid passport.

Which was probably all that Felix Grey carried by way of legal documentation. As with all things relating to him, there are few certainties. If he arrived by boat, which is likely, he would also have completed his disembarkation card which, of course, no longer exists. Other than the fact that he had a son who was 19 years old at the time of the murder of Thomas Bates, and that he claims to have been having a drink with him at an unverified location on the day of the crime, it is difficult to piece together his life. It is probable that lax record-keeping has made any certainty about him even more difficult to attain. In a chilling mirror image of the way in which his son's brief existence has been all but eliminated from popular memory, Felix himself has become equally ghostly.

Countless hours of trawling those records available, with or without recourse to Freedom of Information requests, almost bore fruit. These searches revealed that on 20 August 1959 the Royal Mail Ship (RMS) Ascania docked at Southampton, its final destination, having set sail from Trinidad and picking up in Kingston, Jamaica. On board was a Felix Augustus Gray (sic) who had been born on the first day of June 1925 in Montego Bay. Passenger lists and immigration details are not finely tuned records. My own family has been stamped with both forenames and surnames of varying accuracy as officials from Tilbury to Ellis Island wrestled with strange accents and mystifying globs of consonants from Eastern Europe and Russia. A Gray for a Grey would have been a minor irrelevance.

At 34 years of age in 1959, it is not impossible to suggest that this Gray had a son of 17 at the time. Moreover, the attribution of a man's own middle name to his son is common. The Ascania passenger list contains no such relation but that is just another feature that would have been far from remarkable, with the practice of children joining parents at later dates being commonplace. A Felix Augustus Gray married a Beatrice Shields in Birmingham in July 1973 and Oswald's father claimed to have been drinking with a Phyllis Shields on the night of the murder. But this seems to be nothing other than a tentative coincidence; there remain only a couple of pieces of more compelling evidence, both of which suggest that this groom was not our man.

The electoral rolls of both 1962 and 1965 have a Felix Grey residing at 12, Gordon Road in Lozells, a location which would be entirely consistent with his supposed whereabouts in June 1962. Thereafter, he ceases to appear in any official record – other than the appearance of a Felix Grey in the funeral records of Clarendon, Jamaica in 1964. Did the father, in despair, or possibly shame, at his son's fate, become one of the very few Jamaicans who did, indeed, only reside in the UK temporarily before going back home? The scandal of those treated so disgracefully by the British state, whose papers and identity were literally discarded, make it easy to believe that Felix Grey could have become a non-person, an unknown citizen.

Similarly, the search for details of Oswald's arrival in the UK proved time-consumingly fruitless; the certification of his demise, however, is all too easy to find. The Civil Registration Death Index records with due solemnity that he met his end on 20 November 1962. There also exists the stained sheet outlining the schedule of events of the day of his execution: significantly, he is referred to only in impersonal terms – 'the body', 'the inmate'. The French philosopher Michel Foucault proposed the notion that documents and monuments define us: if that is truly the case, this scant official record of the life of Oswald Grey tells a dispiriting story. This truly was a life forgotten.

As, of course, was that of Thomas Bates, the easy-going, popular tobacconist who fatefully decided not to stroll down the road to the county ground or to take his mom out for a

Saturday evening drink. Whose modest living, adjacent to the number eight bus stop on Lee Bank Road, had already twice been threatened by intruders. Who died up at Steelhouse Lane Hospital being the only person who knew for certain at whose hands he had met his end.

I shall try not to labour the point, but in the course of writing this account, I spoke to scores of people from the city who were alive at the time. Most of them, of course, were either children or young adults. Not one person could recall the event. My sisters, featured at the start of this history, recall nothing of any part of the episode, either the crime or its ghastly outcomes. In conversations with those of Jamaican heritage who regard Birmingham as their home, many expressed astonishment that they had never heard of it. When furnished with details about the circumstantial, if weighty, evidence against Grey and the precipitate nature of his despatch, they are, unsurprisingly, horrified. On the anonymous stretch of urban highway where Thomas's shop once stood, there is nothing – no monument – to mark his brutal, senseless end. In the collective consciousness of the people of Birmingham, neither he nor Oswald Grey have left even the faintest stamp. Our most informed guess is that the son followed the father from their native land and, given the universal lack of any knowledge of either individual, neither left either offspring or incident in England to imprint their existence on anyone who is still alive. It is a truly damning indictment of the state that it was so cavalier in the way that it, too, almost entirely erased them from public record.

Chapter 10

Vile jokes in high places. How a nerdy schoolboy set the standard for British racism.

Steel yourself. What follows is shocking and, what's more, difficult to write. In my defence, and to borrow from two separate sources, the past was a different country and, besides, much of my teenage self is dead.

Jokes.

'What's black and runs down windows?'

'Coondensation.'

'What do you call a coloured bloke in a suit and carrying a briefcase?'

'A chocolate Smartie.'

'There's a coloured bloke and he's sitting there, eating a watermelon and waving his great, big cock around. A bloke comes up to him and asks, "Is that keeping you cool?" and the coloured bloke says, "No. But it sure do keep the flies offa my watermelon."'

Disgracefully, I didn't have to dig too deep into my own early teenage archive to extract these grubby remnants. Unable, of course, to apply any sort of analysis at the time, the reason for my relish for such quips was obvious. I won't disgrace myself further by trying to make excuses.

I moved from the Hebrew School in St Luke's Road, nestling off Lee Bank Road and most definitely Balsall Heath, not Edgbaston, in September 1964. But if it was proper Edgbaston you wanted, that's most certainly where I went.

King Edward's School with its red-brick buildings and verdant playing fields and aping all the trappings of the English public-school system, stood – and still stands – proudly and haughtily next to Birmingham University. It had moved from New Street in the city centre in 1936 in order to enjoy such a relatively bucolic environment. Adjacent to acres of playing fields and abutted by nature reserves, reservoirs and solid brick houses, it is now an establishment into which only the payment of substantial fees permits entrance. Not so in 1964 when, as part of its Direct Grant status, a significant number of places were open to boys (there was a separate girls' school next door) from the city's primary schools. These coveted places were obtained by an entrance examination, over and above the standard 11-plus, which largely asked about the length of time required for given numbers of men to dig holes and how you'd spend your money if you became a millionaire. On top of this were the sort of 'intelligence tests' – see Chapter 7 – designed, by default if not by design, to exclude anyone not attuned to their cultural specificity.

There were no Black boys in my year group, with the exception of one of Anglo-Indian heritage who was, not to put too fine an edge on it, posher than anyone I'd ever known. It is a situation captured perfectly in Jonathan Coe's novel, *The Rotters' Club*, which makes no attempt to disguise the fact that it is modelled on the school. In the book, which is set at a time just after I left in 1971, Steve Richards, the sole Black boy in his year group, endures the incessant, if unwitting, racism of his peers. I am told that there is now some greater diversity in the school's intake, but in 1964, Black boys were a rare commodity. Rarer, even, than Jews.

In 1964, there were about 15 or so of us – and we were very easy to spot. Every school day began with a full school assembly, following a pattern that, as a teacher in later life, I was always childishly tickled to brand as 'a hymn, a prayer and a bollocking'. As the rest of the school filed in to endure this deadening start to the day, Jewish boys were excluded because of its religious content and corralled in a nearby classroom. Here, once the day's notices had been duly delivered to the rest of the school, an insouciant prefect would come along and dully intone what we needed to know. I don't suggest there that there was any malice in this obvious separation, but in terms of being 'othered' – a concept that I wasn't going to get to grips with for another forty years or so – it was a pretty effective measure. The reactions of other boys took place on a continuum from relatively benign envy of our good fortune at missing the awful daily gathering, to the occasional, but painful, barbed and malevolent jibes that have endured through the ages.

So when coon jokes became the order of the day, reflecting, no doubt, the cruel and casual racism that must have peppered conversations in the city, I joined in with great enthusiasm and with a degree of obvious relief that the butt of the jokes were not people like me. My teenage self failed to make any connection between this behaviour and the discomfort I felt about the way in which my own immigrant family spoke in disparaging terms about the 'schwarzers' because, after all, these were just jokes and, besides, everyone told them. And, besides, they weren't about me.

Once again, it was my sisters who rode to the rescue, albeit in somewhat passive roles. The TV sitcom *Friday Night Dinner* captures something of the centrality of that weekly family episode in the lives of Jewish people. By the mid-60s, by which time my mother was remarried and my sisters in early adulthood, it assumed a degree of glamour as they began to bring young men of varying accomplishments, charm and good looks to the table. It was, of course, an open invitation for a precocious and entirely self-unaware brat to show off. And what better way to do this than to regale everyone with the latest schoolyard jokes. About coons and darkies.

Most of the newbies, concerned, no doubt, not to dampen their chances with their prospective inamorata, were either vaguely non-committal in their responses or, on occasion, would attempt to top my efforts with one from their own repertoire. Until the game-changer came on the scene.

I cannot recall which of these hugely entertaining witticisms I wheeled out on the occasion in question, but the response brought my clowning to a juddering halt. Instead of the usual quiet compliance or jolly rejoinder, the evening's dinner guest fixed me calmly and with a stare that was a mixture of surprise and disappointment. He didn't gently roll his eyes or grin sheepishly and he certainly didn't attempt to trump my efforts. The gist of his comments, delivered in a measured and biting way, was this: discriminatory 'jokes' of this sort weren't funny, they demeaned the victim and the teller and, really, really, I ought to know better. My younger sister attempted to throw me a lifeline by pointing out – truthfully – that I knew a thing or two about putting up with prejudicial behaviour, only to be politely shot down by the observation that this was even more reason for me to reconsider my thoughts and actions. Like everyone else at the table, I was taken aback as my inflated, self-important view of my obvious hilarity was so sharply punctured.

I'm sure the topic of conversation must have been changed as we survived the evening. As for the young man himself, I am fairly certain that this was his last appearance and that he wasn't to be a significant feature in the lives of either of the belles on show. Although I have a vague recollection of what he looked like, unfortunately, that is all I have left of him. And I say that this is unfortunate because his forthright and, on reflection, brave words had their desired effect. Tentatively at first and then, with growing confidence, I showed my quiet disapproval of such jokes until such time as I developed the self-assurance to upbraid the tellers myself. Regrettably, it's an ongoing project.

It is worth reinforcing the point about where, precisely, this discourse of unchallenged racism was coming from. King Edward's School was not a back-street primary in central Birmingham, which is where I had come from and where the first wave of Black immigrants had developed their own unrefined ways of dealing with such comments. This was in the belly of the respectable beast. I hope my schoolfellows look back on their actions with similar embarrassment; among their number are a former cabinet minister, eminent broadcasters, scientists, senior academics, novelists and a squint through the alumni list reveals any number of CBEs, OBEs and similar awards. If the likes of us were happy to make such jokes, this has to tell us something of the society in which they had become so ubiquitous. And why, as well, the hanging of a young Black man in our city barely merited notice.

This miserable state of affairs goes some way to explaining how the entirely non-attributable story of Oswald Grey spending his final days on earth hand-jiving and limbo-dancing must have gained sufficient traction to bear repeating. The vile assumptions that underpin such obvious fiction have their roots in the 'jokes' and jibes that must have been an everyday part of life on the factory floor, bus garage and hospital ward. They would have enlivened break times in offices, department stores and, yes, boys' grammar schools. In the case of my own, that school had the dubious distinction of having produced one of the most notorious of racists – albeit it is difficult to imagine him ever invoking widespread merriment and laughter in the tearoom or behind the bike sheds.

The name of John Enoch Powell adorns the honours board at King Edward's School, Birmingham, which he left in 1930. On the back of a glittering academic record, he went on to study at Trinity College, Cambridge. Once there, his intellectual prowess gathered even greater momentum, earning double-starred firsts in Latin and Greek. Apparently unfulfilled by such accomplishment, in later life he studied Urdu at the University of London, a course he undertook to better place himself for the public post he most craved – that of Viceroy of India. As if his credentials as a polyglot could be further enhanced, he also became proficient in German, Welsh, Modern Greek and Portuguese as he enjoyed a variety of senior positions in various civil and military settings. He deployed his extraordinary abilities when serving with great distinction as an intelligence officer during the Second World War. He was an astonishingly talented individual.

History has now defined him almost exclusively by his 'Rivers of Blood' speech, made at a meeting of the Conservative Political Centre in Birmingham in 1968. He delivered his infamous words in the Midland Hotel, not far from where had gone to school, and where, according to Simon Heffer's forensically detailed biography, his enduringly serious demeanour earned him the nickname of Scowelly-Powelly. One of his teachers remembers him as an 'austere' figure whom one never saw 'standing up against a wall with his hands in his pockets, just talking'. Powell's asceticism and scholarly nature are, apart from his irredeemable racism, the staunch hallmarks of his character. In the 1995 biographical TV documentary, *Odd Man Out*, he admits to the fact that he 'had no social life as an undergraduate'. His remarks throughout the film are mechanically humourless, his responses to questions about his political career oddly robotic. An unattributed comment from a colleague talks of him being 'driven mad by the remorselessness of his own logic' and it is fair to say that, although not without ambition – he freely admitted to having his eye on the prize of becoming Prime Minister – Powell was a man who marched to the beat of his very own drum.

On 20 April 1968, he was the Conservative MP for Wolverhampton South-West, some twenty miles away from the venue where he delivered his speech. The transcript, easily accessible online, is disturbing. Not all of the speech was filmed. Although the lines in which he rails that 'we must be mad, literally mad, as a nation to be permitting the annual inflow of some 50,000 dependants' along with his final vision of a Britain like 'the River Tiber flowing with much blood' have become notorious because of their visibility on film, there are other, equally alarming, but less familiar, extracts. He illuminates his commentary with anecdotes from constituents. One declared that he wouldn't be happy until he had seen his well-educated children settled overseas, so concerned was he that 'in this country in 15 or 20 years' time, the Black man will have the whip hand over the white man'. Another tells of how her refusal to let rooms in her large house to immigrant families has led to her being assailed on her way to the shops by 'charming, wide-grinning picanninnies' who 'cannot speak English, but one word they know. "Racialist" they chant'. Not to expose such episodes, Powell insisted, would constitute a 'great betrayal'.

That Powell had chosen the centre of Birmingham as the place to make his speech could not have been a matter of chance. Sandwiched between the city centre and his Wolverhampton constituency, five miles to the north of Lee Bank Road, was the borough of Smethwick. Four years earlier it had found itself at the centre of a national controversy.

Peter Griffiths was a local primary headteacher. His academic accomplishments were not in the same stratosphere as those of Powell, but he had gained a master's degree in education at Birmingham University on completion of his national service. He was charming, forthright and personable and in the October election of 1964, he stood for the Conservative party in Smethwick against the incumbent, Patrick Gordon Walker, who was the prospective Foreign Secretary in the confidently predicted Labour government. Smethwick was, historically, a safe Labour seat, once held for the party, in a historical quirk, by Oswald Mosely between 1926-31, before he went on to found the British Union of Fascists. In 1964, Harold Wilson's Labour did, indeed, win the election, but, against all trends, Griffiths defeated Gordon Walker.

Contrary to folkloric belief, there was never an election leaflet in Smethwick bearing the slogan 'If you want a nigger for a neighbour, vote Labour' although there were those that came very close to doing so. Leaflets displaying these words, often unattributed and usually crudely produced with grammatical and spelling errors, had appeared elsewhere in the country. Moreover, there are plenty of individual recollections of the use of the slogan as well as other rhymes and ditties of equal offensiveness. There is footage to show that it appeared, painted in large white letters, on a wall in a Smethwick street and, when confronted by its message, Peter Griffiths resolutely refused to distance himself from it. If 'success' has many fathers, there are plenty who lay claim to its provenance, from the self-styled godfather of the British right, Colin Jordan, to the daughter of Griffiths' election agent, Cressida Dickens, who claims, at nine years of age, to have quietly chanted it an organising meeting in her home – attended by Enoch Powell – to the great approval of all present.

Griffiths' energetic campaign, focussing on the well-worn fears about housing shortages and jobs being stolen, resulted in a 7.2% swing away from Labour, furnishing him with a majority of 1,774. The months that followed were turbulent. The residents of Marshall Street in Smethwick mounted a vigorous campaign demanding that the council buy up vacant properties on the street and forbid the sale of any of them to 'coloured' residents. Early in 1965, they took their case to the newly installed minister for housing, Richard Crossman. They did so with the official support of members of Smethwick council and of Griffiths himself. In a moment of TV footage that might have been almost comical were it not for the dire context, a Councillor Jackson, replete with unfortunate Hitleresque moustache, is stunned into dull, bovine silence when asked where the coloured population was to live if such de-facto colour bars were to be implemented.

Crossman gave the petitioners short shrift, but not before their actions had generated huge publicity. In a genuinely extraordinary episode, American civil rights activist, Malcolm X, visited the borough to express his solidarity with the Black and Asian communities there. A blue plaque commemorates the visit, which took place only nine days before his assassination at the Audubon Ballroom in New York on 21 February. It is an incident that, despite coming to light in more recent times, went almost entirely unnoticed when it occurred. Local filmmaker, Stephen Page, who has unearthed a good deal of footage and commentary of the event, noted that he 'spoke to Black community leaders who were active at the time and they didn't realise he had been to the town'. Avtar Singh Jouhl, then secretary of the Indian Workers' Association, who, in defiance of their unwelcome presence in a local pub, had a drink with Malcolm X, may wish to take issue with this observation, but it remains fair to say that the visit could easily have become forgotten history without the efforts of Page and others.

Four months later in June 1965, George Newey and 15 others of like mind, met in the Chapel Tavern on the corner of Great Charles Street and Ludgate Hill, now demolished and lying where the Queensway tunnel allows drivers, on a good day, to slide through the tangle of the city centre. On that June evening, Newey and his pals were present to form the first British chapter of the Ku Klux Klan. Newey was no Enoch Powell when it came to political rhetoric. 'We must fight the nig-nog', he proclaims to his ardent followers. We were being invaded, he told the potential founders of the new master race, by 'the scum and the throw-outs of their stinking black countries'. TV journalist, Reg Harcourt, courteous but bemused, asks him if there will be cross-burning. Mr Newey is unfazed. If these can take place 'somewhere private and in the open' then they most certainly will occur.

There was nothing remotely amusing about his response when, some days later, Mrs Ruby Henry did, indeed, awake to find a burning cross nailed to her front door in Albert Street – the same street where Oswald Grey claimed he had been partying on the night of Thomas Bates's death – within walking distance of the Chapel Tavern. It is Harcourt, working for ITV News, who is delegated to cover the story the next day in incongruously glorious sunshine. Neighbours and their children mill around, demonstrably star-struck by the fact that the telly had come to their street. Ruby Henry is obviously shocked and scared as she tells him that although she and her family have lived there for four years, she doesn't 'think I'll stop here any longer'. She has sent her children away and is working hard to hold back tears as she talks. Harcourt speaks to her neighbours, a mixed group with Black people in the majority. Most of them are convinced that this is the work of organised racists, probably inspired by the news of the Newey's band of brothers.

At the end of the following Spring, the country went to the polls again. Prime Minister Harold Wilson, hidebound by a tiny majority of four, was certain that another election would furnish him with a more secure set of numbers and his judgement turned out to be sound: he now sat on a plump cushion of a 96-point advantage. In Smethwick, Griffiths faced a candidate deliberately chosen for his charismatic presence, the actor Andrew Faulds. Along with some concerted anti-racist activity organised by Jouhl and student campaigners, Faulds' decision to tackle the racism of Griffiths in an uncompromising way resulted in a reversal of the 1964 result. A 7.6% swing back to Labour rewarded him with a majority of 3,490. Although a temporary setback for Griffiths, the Conservative party did not consider itself to have been defiled by touching his particular pitch. After a spell as a minor academic, he returned to politics as MP for Portsmouth North, a seat he held from 1979 until 1997. After his flirtation with notoriety, this later period of service is notable only for its numbing anonymity. He died in 2013.

For poor Patrick Gordon Walker, things got no better in the weeks following his defeat to Peter Griffiths. Shortly after the installation of the Labour government, Harold Wilson granted a peerage to Reginald Sorensen, the sitting MP for the safe seat of Leyton in east London. This was the time for Gordon Walker to get back on the horse and resume his parliamentary career. Up against him was the Conservative candidate, Ronald Buxton, who endured a fleeting and undistinguished political career, enlivened only by the few months of success he went on to enjoy between January of 1965 and March 1966. Heartened, no doubt, by the successful tactics of Griffiths and his followers in Smethwick, Colin Jordan, the self-styled cartoon fuhrer of Britain's microscopic National Socialist Movement, decided that this was to be his chance for a moment in the sun.

Birmingham born, Jordan, who died in 2009 at the age of 85, is part of a long and discreditable line of British fascists who conveniently forget their comfortable background and privilege and go on to infest public life, claiming to say the unsayable on behalf of the ordinary man in the street. Privately educated at Warwick School and Cambridge, Jordan had hung around every group of right-leaning undesirables since forming the White Defence League from an inherited property in Notting Hill in 1956. On 7 January 1965, he led a group of his fellow stormtroopers into a public meeting at Leyton Town Hall – the episode is captured on a BBC *Panorama* clip – in an attempt to seize the platform. Before he and, in the words of the BBC voice-over, his 'group of burly racialists' were ejected from the meeting by stewards – all parties resolutely continuing to smoke during the fracas – Jordan became the recipient of a decent right-hander from the future Defence Secretary and Chancellor of the Exchequer, Denis Healey. 'Why don't you go and live with the Blacks if you like them so much?' Jordan demanded of Gordon Walker, a limp rejoinder still to be heard from those oafishly upholding his tradition.

Despite his ignominious exit from the Town Hall, Jordan had struck the chord of racism that chimed throughout the by-election. In a close mirror of events in Smethwick, an 8.7% swing to the Conservatives produced a tiny minority of 205 in their favour. Their period in office was brief. Fourteen months later in March 1966, Gordon Walker regained the seat with a majority of 8,646. Analyses in the years that have followed have attributed his defeat in 1965 to resentment from Labour supporters at an imposed candidate and to a low turnout, although at 57.7% this looks extremely healthy by modern by-election standards. There may be truth in this, but Gordon Walker and Labour seemed to be slow learners when it came to confronting racism head-on and building alliances with those who could aid them in doing so.

Whenever race and immigration found its way onto the electoral agenda, Labour found itself wriggling with discomfort. Its stance in the mid-1960s set the tone for the party's timidity on the issues for the next seven decades. Ideologically opposed as its parliamentarians and its membership may have been to racism, there lingered the abiding nag that opposition to immigration played well with the electorate. Another of Labour's future doyens, Roy Hattersley, whose prowess at fisticuffs remains unreported, won the seat of Birmingham Sparkbrook, in 1964. It was and remains – albeit renamed as Sparkbrook and Small Heath – an archetypal inner-city constituency and Hattersley went on to represent it ably for 33 years. Nevertheless, only weeks after first taking his parliamentary seat, he expressed the concern that 'unrestricted immigration can only produce additional problems, additional suffering and additional hardship unless some kind of limitation is imposed and continued'.

All of which is by way of arguing that by the time Enoch Powell stood up at the Midland Hotel in April 1968, in front of the cameras and with his eye on the biggest prize in British politics, he may well have anticipated a degree of opprobrium coming his way, but could calculate that a forthright and provocative stance on race was going to do him more good than harm. In the immediate term, he was entirely correct, yet even he may have been taken aback by how quickly he was proved to be surfing the tide of the zeitgeist.

Three days after his invocation of the rivers of blood that would flow through the country, a bizarre display took place in central London. Organised groups of unionised workers marched on parliament to express their support for 'good old Enoch'. Builders, dockers and meat porters made their way to the House, rumbustiously declaring support for their hero of the hour. Once there, they were warmly greeted by ebullient, moustachioed Tory icon and knight of the realm, Sir Gerald Nabarro, MP for South Worcestershire. Nabarro, full to the brim with his characteristic bonhomie, posed cheerfully with these horny-handed sons of labour with whom he shared common ground. His presence could hardly have been deemed a surprise. In one of the many egregious outbursts for which his media appearances were notorious, he had bluffly asked the audience on BBC radio's *Any Questions?* on 5 April 1963 how they might 'feel if your daughter wanted to marry a big buck nigger with the prospect of coffee-coloured grandchildren?' Broadcast live and in the days prior to the delay that might be imposed on such rough comment, his query was expunged from the repeat of the programme – even the less delicate susceptibilities of a 1963 audience might have sensed that a line had been crossed. Nonetheless, this was far from the good knight's last appearance on similar panels; such colourful sentiments were still regarded as precious good copy.

There can be no underplaying the fact that the workers' demonstrations were disorientating. The *Daily Mirror* captured the perplexing situation by talking of 'the strange spectacle of London dockers marching to parliament to express their support for a Tory politician'. The forays to Westminster were not, however, quite the spontaneous uprisings they appeared to be. As with any such event, there must be organisers and key figures: those on 23 April 1968 had genuine form when it came to right-wing activity, even though their influence was skated over at the time.

Leading the delegation of meat porters was Dennis 'Big Dan' Harmston, who was a member of the Union Movement, formerly the British Union of Fascists led by Oswald Mosley, for whom Harmston acted as bodyguard. The dockers had two people at the helm, Pat Duig and Harry Pearman. The former was also a member of the Union Movement and the latter was a leading figure in Moral Rearmament, an anti-communist body dedicated to establishing 'fundamental values'. As tiny as such grouplets were, they were indicative of the move towards organised racist activity of the sort that had crept into the light at the Chapel Tavern in Birmingham in 1965. The *Mirror's* editorial was suitably concerned, as one might expect a Labour-leaning journal to be, by the protests, but directed its ire at what it saw as Powell's opportunism. He was, according to the paper's editorial, 'an educated fanatic ... guilty of an act of mischief'.

Mischievous or not, he became, for a time, the most recognised politician in the country. The right-leaning author, Douglas Murray, claims that Tory grandee Michael Heseltine was of the opinion that if Powell has stood for the leadership of his party in the aftermath of his speech, he would have won by a landslide – and if he had stood to be Prime Minister by a 'national landslide'. Yet Powell continued to be driven by that irrepressible remorselessness of logic that often played out in erratic ways. His parliamentary voting record on the issues of the day – including the early wrangling about Britain's place in Europe – was so unpredictable that it would have had the bookies' heads spinning. Popular in the country he may well have been; reliable in terms of his party's grandees and paymasters, he was not. His light blazed fiercely but briefly yet by the early 70s his political career, to cite Murray further, 'did not merely falter but (he) remained in the political wilderness for the remaining decades of his life'.

Powell died in 1998 aged 85 having stamped himself

indelibly on the history of modern British politics. Although his moment of greatest notoriety occurred in the centre of the city of his birth, there doesn't appear to be any evidence that Powell ever thought of himself as a proud Brummie. In terms of his association with King Edward's School, it is difficult to discern how that institution might feel about its association with him: attempts on my behalf to find out were met with dull, official silence. On a personal level, however, I have reason to express some gratitude towards him.

In October 1969, I had just started my A levels. Powell had been invited to address a selective audience at the school as part of a fund-raising effort to enhance its already extensive sports facilities. By this time, thanks to the Friday night dinner guest who had set me on my way, I had completed a full 180-degree turn on the coon jokes, become informed and enraged about apartheid and been suitably appalled by Powell's speech at The Midland. Across the road from the school was the University of Birmingham and in the university was the Students' Union, or Guild. Some of us decided, very properly, that people there needed to know about this planned event and our information was gladly received. We thought some local knowledge about side-doors and the geography of the buildings might turn out to be equally useful. My life as an active political being had commenced.

On 4 October, the front page of the *Birmingham Post* informed its readers that the police had held 'five at Powell meeting' along with a picture of a pedestrian-looking copper apprehending an equally static protester. The paper reports on a degree of almost genteel rowdiness at the meeting, prior to the rejection of the intruders. A Mr Timothy Davies, an old boy of the school, had shouted at Mr Powell and had been rewarded by being 'slapped very hard across the face' by another attendee. The *Post* describes how 'a middle-aged man with a goatee beard and dressed in a lounge suit ...shouted at Mr Powell "Enoch, you're an intellectual cretin" (and) was promptly dragged from the room by stewards'.

But this restrained, almost mannerly, episode is important. Just a few years earlier, the Birmingham known briefly to Oswald Grey would have been alien and unwelcoming. His life, as far as those legislators and jurors who were to consider the accusations against him were concerned, was that of a second-class citizen. Yet, if one were to take the words of a pre-1968 Enoch Powell at face value, that would have been a position that the politician would have found utterly repellent.

In the early hours of the morning of 28 July 1959, the member for Wolverhampton, South West, had risen to speak in a parliamentary debate that had started three hours earlier. The House was considering the disturbing affair of the massacre of eleven prisoners at a forced labour camp in Hola, Kenya, under British rule, in January of that year. Powell appears to be genuinely discomfited by some of the language used in the debate. In particular, he is disturbed by an apparent presumption by some of his colleagues that these prisoners had what was coming to them. He is vehement in his insistence that the lives of the eleven victims were worth no less than those of other men. 'It is a fearful doctrine,' he insisted, 'to stand in judgement of a fellow human being and to say 'because he is such-and-such' therefore the consequences of what others do to him are diminished in any way.' Denis Healey, he of the right-hander in Leyton Town Hall, called it 'the greatest parliamentary speech I ever heard'. Yet for all of this show of humanity and compassion, there is no recorded commentary of Powell's reaction to the cursory trial and flimsy evidence that saw a young Black man executed in his own city three years later. His commendable advocacy for Black men thousands of miles from Birmingham was not matched by any similar concern for a young man much closer to home.

There is a wretched tale to tell here. It is one about lives, like those of Oswald Grey, that do not seem to matter, even where they have been lived on the doorsteps of those to whom we might look for moral guidance and leadership. Six more young men, aged between 21 and 26, followed Oswald Grey to the gallows before the last two of them, Peter Allen and Gwynne Evans – Harry Allen's final victim – were hanged for the murder of John West, simultaneously but in different locations, on 13 August 1964. Their botched and clumsy crime saw them leave the scene with a watch and a bankbook worth about £10. In this, as in their lives characterised by sporadic employment and bungling petty crime, Allen and Evans resembled dozens whom the state saw fit to kill as punishment. Many of them were poorly educated, itinerant and lacking in social skills; often their crimes were committed when drunk or just plain angry. They would have cut sorry figures in front of respectable juries whose imaginations would have been inflamed by the rhetoric of trained orators. Trained orators who may well have traded coon jokes as they relaxed together in chambers. After all, everyone else did.

When they went into court, those charged with pleading the cause of these disadvantaged but unprepossessing young men often look to have gone about it less enthusiastically than they should have done. Discourses of racism went unchallenged in the bar rooms of Britain whether those bars were in high streets or the High Court. Oswald Grey would, therefore, have been doubly disadvantaged. Not only was he part of a shady world of simple ne'er-do-wells, he was coloured. He was the other, a Jamaican immigrant. Circumstances stacked ever higher to negatively influence how he was perceived by a jury of his so-called peers. His was a life that was disposable on a number of counts. It was on this burgeoning perception of the Black man as an unwelcome irritant, the acceptable butt of jokes and a dangerous outsider, that Powell chose to build his scandalous career.

Have you heard the one about the grinning, hand-jiving, limbo-dancing Jamaican waiting to be hanged?

Don't bother. It's not remotely funny.

Footnote. New Street: home to inglorious episodes

Birmingham's New Street might possibly have held a place deep in the stony heart of John Enoch Powell, as it does, one way or another, for many Brummies. Although his school days there do not seem to have been filled with laughter and merriment, they were the platform on which he built his multi-faceted career. It was also the street where he delivered the noxious speech which stamped his name, albeit rather ingloriously, on the history of decades to come. For many residents of the city, New Street will also bear the mark of the IRA attack on an underground boozer, The Tavern in the Town, in November 1974, killing 21 people and injuring a further 182. As a favoured haunt of young people, especially on a Thursday night which is when the bombings occurred, I knew it well.

The narrow doorway of the Tavern, from where the steps led down to the pub itself, is nestled next door to the Odeon cinema, which now occupies the territory of Powell's alma mater, King Edward's School before it moved to Edgbaston in 1937. It was at a gig in this venue in 1976 that Eric Clapton, widely revered as one of the world's foremost rock guitarists, spewed out a stream of racist abuse, at the same time as invoking Powell's name and beliefs as the inspiration for his bilious comments.

There is no footage of the incident and no authoritative recording of what Clapton said on the evening of 5 August 1976, but there is sufficient similarity among the reports of his outburst to form an unequivocally clear impression of the thrust of his comments.

Having asked any foreigners in the audience to identify themselves, Clapton expresses the view that he wants them neither in the room nor in his country. He goes on to advocate a vote for our man, Enoch, in order to stop Britain from becoming a black colony. Enoch was most definitely right. Fucking bastard black wogs, coons (and, for reasons best known to himself, Saudis) along with fucking Jamaicans and Arabs, should have it made clear to them that they're not welcome here, in a white country for white people. He concludes by asking what has happened to us, for fuck's sake?

This edited, paraphrased version makes ugly reading, but Clapton has never denied making the comments and although an apology of sorts has been offered, he made it using the lame excuse of so many miscreants who hide behind the effects of personal difficulties and a struggle with addictive substances. In Lili Fini Zanuck's 2017 documentary, *Eric Clapton: A Life in 12 Bars*, the guitarist admits that he 'did really offensive things', describing himself as 'a full-tilt racist' at the time. He continues, rather cryptically, to blame his behaviour of the 'Arab invasion' and suggesting that 'there was this sort of thing in the air in the early 1970s' and although he admits 'it was an awful thing to do', concludes by observing that 'I think it's funny actually'.

Clapton's claim that there was something in the air in Birmingham – and elsewhere – in the mid-1970s and that Powell's words and actions had contributed to this febrile, unpleasant atmosphere, have some credibility. As the putrid 'jokes' at the start of this chapter illustrate, the expression of naked racism was rife and usually unchallenged. Many individuals, myself included, are right to look back, shudder and offer an open apology. The words of contrition from the great guitarist, however, ring less than true: he went on to take his crusade for personal liberty to bizarre lengths as the end of 2020 approached.

The government's efforts to curb the pandemic had been put in place, according to his song *Stand and Deliver*, to 'put the fear on you, but not a word you heard was true'. If you comply with these restraints on your personal freedom, you have to ask yourself whether 'you want to be a free man, or do you want to be a slave?'

A global rock star is, of course, entitled to his misguided opinions as any of us. The purpose of this footnote is nothing more than to revive a New Street memory that brackets together a racist politician and a racist musician and put them in the same time and place in history. Oswald Augustus Grey, long gone by the time of the New Street of the Powell speech and the Clapton rant, is part of the foreword to the story of these repellent men.

Chapter 11

Sixty years on: Black boy dies in Lee Bank. Of course he does.

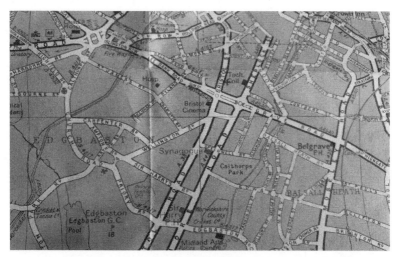

Birmingham 1962

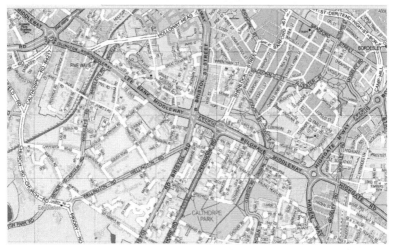

Birmingham 2021

Late summer, 2021. We are out of lockdown and I am on Lee Bank Middleway. The scene of the crime for which Oswald Grey was convicted can no longer be identified, obliterated by the concrete anonymity of bland redevelopment. Traffic streams along. The stretch of road where Thomas Bates ran the fags and paper shop is just a section of urban highway, located between two sets of traffic lights where boy-racers rev and brake ferociously by turns. In December 2017, Lee Bank hit the national news when the car of one such boy careered across the carriageway, killing six people as it went. The scene of horror and carnage generated headlines, outrage and opprobrium towards the guilty driver. A prompt, open inquest followed. Four of the victims were British people of Asian descent; there was a flash-Harry in a top-range Audi, a taxi driver making his way home and a couple returning from a night out. It was a crime of the times – and not one to be buried in a meagre 117 words.

Similarly, the murder of Anthony Sargeant, a Black Brummie and the self-styled 'King of Lee Bank', who was shot across the Bristol Road in Rickman Drive in September 2018, prompted widespread national coverage. A father of eight, Sargeant provided good copy. There were plentiful pictures of him proudly lining up with his children, having a drink with his old mom in a social club, enjoying the beach in St Lucia and cradling the trophy won by the Sunday League side he ran. Sargeant had another string to his bow, performing as a rapper and going by the name of Scally Jones. There are numerous tributes to him on social media pages and any number of people happy to be identified as his associates, going on the record to appreciate his contribution to the society in which he lived and worked. There are, unsurprisingly, unavoidable suggestions that anyone who was the victim of a targeted drive-by shooting may not have lived an entirely saintly existence, and this suspicion was enhanced when his brother, Andre, was handed a short prison sentence six months after Anthony's death. In possession of an illegal weapon, Andre was chased by police down Belgrave Middleway and, no doubt because there was no number 8 bus in sight onto which he could conveniently hop, was detained and arrested. Even this brief escapade warranted more attention than the dismissive, peremptory treatment of Oswald Grey.

My personal pilgrimage to these places of my birth, childhood and primary schooling bears all the hallmarks of such journeys. Places are the same but different, less imposing yet fascinating as they reveal the cultural and societal upheavals of the past six decades.

The Hebrew School on St Luke's Road was eventually demolished in 2018, although, given the sturdiness of its build, it wouldn't have gone down without a fight. There is still an abattoir on the corner of Wrentham Street, but as it's for halal slaughter, no schoolchild will thrill to the parade of thundering, condemned porkers trundling to their end. Besides, it is nothing more than a disappointingly functional-looking set of dull, industrial outbuildings. Abutting nearby Kent Street, where we would file in for our weekly school swim, to be then crammed double in tiny changing cubicles, is the city's Gay Village, looking a touch forlorn as it awaits the full return of nightlife and high jinks.

Walking from St Luke's Road, currently in the throes of major development, going across to Belgravia Close, formerly Varna Road, requires noisy navigation across Lee Bank Middleway, now built for traffic, not the quick purchase of ten Park Drive cigarettes. The Close bears no indication of its once salacious past but, regrettably, parts of it still looks in need of some love and attention. What had once seemed a trek across Calthorpe Park is just a stroll of few minutes, to where Edward Road and Mary Street mirror inner-city streets anywhere in the country. To take such a walk as a middle-aged white man in 2021 is to be treated with the same invisible disregard as, I suspect, a group of grubby nine-year-olds would have been sixty years earlier.

There may be the vestiges of familiarity but this is a different Birmingham from that of 1962. A stroll through the city centre, even in just-about post-Covid times, is to witness a city that, on the surface at least, is comfortable with its wide range of heritage and culture. The last complete census in 2011 revealed that nearly one in ten people in England and Wales living as a couple were in an inter-ethnic relationship. It is easy to believe that this figure could even be an under-estimate when it comes to Birmingham, judging by a walk around the Bull Ring and the adjoining market area. All the same, nobody in their right mind would pretend that the city represents a cosy, warm melting-pot of integration, and, as such, it has been a target for lazy commentators over the years.

In October 2012, Birmingham's *Sunday Mercury* ran a front-page story under the headline, 'The areas of Birmingham that are no-go for white people'. The white people in question were working-class and the article is smattered with anonymous comments from unidentified contributors and unsubstantiated anecdotal observation. It was a back-to-the-future moment; the complaints were about poor housing and diminishing facilities, just as they were when delegations from Lambeth and Smethwick tramped to Westminster with their complaints in previous decades. It was left to the chairman of Birmingham Central Mosque, located a few yards up the road from Lee Bank, to set the record straight. 'If the white working class in Birmingham do feel betrayed,' suggested Dr Mohammed Naseem, 'then it is the fault of successive Governments, it has nothing to do with race or immigration or anything like that.'

For egregious comment, however, the efforts of the *Mercury* fade into dust in comparison with the musings of Steven Emerson on Fox News in January 2015. Emerson, who describes himself on his website as an 'internationally recognised expert on terrorism and national security', revealed to an aghast presenter that the entire city of Birmingham in England was a no-go area subject to Sharia Law and patrolled by a vigilante security force. He was forced to apologise, but not before being subjected to an onslaught of social media comment from Brummies, almost all of which adopted a tone of comic derision. My own favourites were the tweeting of a piece of Islamic art juxtaposed to a photo of the Spaghetti Junction interchange as proof of evil forces at work. Then there was the almost inevitable picture of a Mecca bingo hall as further confirmation of a none too surreptitious take-over.

This lunatic fringe apart, and allowing for the fact that there are suburbs where some ethnic groups form a clear majority, a fair assessment would be that the city represents as positive a model of integration as anywhere. The explicit, if unthinking, racism of the 1950s and 60s has dissipated and it would be a particularly obtuse, or dimly brave, individual who tried out a coon joke in anything but the most private of settings.

From Lee Bank, it's just a three-mile journey up to Winson Green Prison, now HMP Birmingham. Gone is the resemblance to a cross between a Victorian asylum and a mock-medieval fortress. The frontage could now be mistaken for the entrance to the premises of an energy company, keen to demonstrate that one of its principal shareholders knew someone who was once an architect. However, its aesthetic impact is the very least of its concerns as an institution. Behind its confident, futuristic façade is a place with a hellish recent history.

In 2011, the Coalition Government, for whom the privatisation of formerly public-owned services was an article of faith, handed control of the prison to the private company G4S. If one were to be charitable to the Home Secretary of the time, Theresa May, the full litany of G4S's catastrophic failures was yet to completely unfold. Over the next few years, the company oversaw bullying and mismanagement of jaw-dropping proportions at an immigration centre at Gatwick and a young offenders' establishment in Medway. They haplessly overcharged the Ministry of Justice for the electronic tagging of prisoners and, famously, failed to deliver on its promise of supplying 'elite security personnel' for the London Olympics and were bailed out by the army. This catalogue of catastrophe – and these are just the edited highlights – might be amusing if it were not for the fact that the company's fecklessness threatened the lives and safety of thousands of people.

In 2018, following riots at Winson Green, the government was forced to return control to the prison service and in late July 2018, Her Majesty's Chief Inspector of Prisons, Peter Clarke, led an unannounced inspection. The tone and language he then used in his report were chosen carefully to ensure that there could be absolutely no ambiguity about the judgements he had reached. Following an earlier initial visit after the riots, Clarke had been gratified to note 'a determination to recover and rebuild'. Some months later, however, as a result of the surprise inspection, he was duty bound to observe that 'far from recovering, the prison had deteriorated dramatically and was in an appalling state'. Staff turnover was rapid and 'control in the prison was tenuous'. He went on to report that 'prisoners were living in squalor (and) little was being done to adequately occupy individuals' before repeating, for avoidance of doubt, his view that 'the prison was in an appalling state'. Throughout the report, Clarke returns to the issue of safety, for both staff and inmates, in a place where 71% of prisoners felt in danger.

The ethnic composition of those inmates would be entirely different from that recognised, however tangentially, by Oswald Grey in the late summer and autumn of 1962. Prison officer Robert Douglas, he of the hilarious 'turning white' jape in Chapter 2, talked of one cell of West Indian prisoners and it would be fair to assume that imprisonment of such individuals would have been comparatively rare, given their numbers within the wider community. Prisons at that time, along with most public institutions, would not have included ethnicity in their record-keeping. In 1961, the Census asked questions about migrant status for the first time and the figures revealed some 415,000 such respondents. This represented significantly less than 1% of the population, although closer academic scrutiny at Warwick University has since suggested that this may be a slight underestimate with those coming to the UK to be united with families going unrecorded as migrants. It is difficult to be exact as to whether that 1% was an accurate reflection of the ethnic make-up of the city at the time or to know if this was reflected by the number of inmates, but the figures at the time of Peter Clarke's inspection are clear.

Over a third of those in Winson Green were from backgrounds not classified as White British. Of those, some 13% of the overall prison population were Asian or British Asian and 21% were Black or mixed Black heritage. These figures represent a slight increase on the national average of BAME prisoners which, according to a Prison Reform Trust report of October 2020, stands at 26%. The Trust calculates that if the country's prison population were to mirror its ethnic composition, some 9,000 fewer people would be incarcerated – the equivalent of 12 average-sized institutions. In 2017, Labour MP for Tottenham, David Lammy – see chapter 7 for the story of his mother's determination to succeed as an immigrant – headed an independent review into the treatment of, and outcomes for, Black, Asian and Minority Ethnic individuals in the criminal justice system. His findings were disturbing but would have come as nothing of a shock to anyone even passingly familiar with events on the ground.

Lammy deplored the fact that in the decade up to 2016, the proportion of Black teenagers in youth prisons had risen from 25% to 41%. When it came to trust between Black communities and the police, his comments contribute to a truism that finds voice in the starkly, damning judgement of the Prison Reform Trust that 'you get a worse deal from our criminal justice system if you're from an ethnic minority'. The figures relating to the rate at which Black people are summarily stopped by police vary, but an authoritative piece of research by the London School of Economics in 2018 revealed that, overall, Black people were eight times more likely to be the victim of this than whites. The same publication went on to assert that, 'while studies have repeatedly shown that stop and search has no impact on knife crime and serious violence, it selectively criminalises Black people and those from other minority groups for offences that are largely ignored in other contexts'. It concludes with the unequivocal comment that 'whatever the intention might be, stop and search is a driver of discrimination'.

As telling as such commentary may be, for most Black people it serves only to confirm what they already know. While there is news value in high-profile athletes, public figures and accomplished professionals being pulled over for being in possession of a sleek motor car, such discrimination is sutured into the lives of thousands of Black people going about their mundane, daily business.

Nathaniel Jones lives in Chelmsley Wood, a part of Birmingham that not even its most ardent advocates could paint as a pastoral idyll. In October 2020, the *Daily Mirror* ran a story about how, by Nathaniel's calculations, his impromptu encounters with the police ran into the high hundreds. 'I had no criminal record, I was a good lad,' he told the paper. 'To be stopped and searched that many times used to get me frustrated.' He talks of how he 'never used to like the police because I couldn't really understand and grasp why they would treat me differently to my white friends.' Jones is a youth worker, determined to enhance his qualifications to be able to train young people to deal effectively with their interactions with West Midlands Police. If he's still the object of their attentions, it doesn't take much to imagine the treatment of other young Black men. Or that of Oswald Grey when he was arrested in June 1962.

Despite the suspicion thrust upon them as potential

perpetrators, Black men remain more likely to be a victim of crime than anyone else. Figures released from the Greater London Authority, from its survey of crime in the capital from 2014- 19, showed that in terms of violent crime, Black men and boys – not including those of either Asian or mixed heritage – accounted for 25% of victims. In terms of the involvement of young Black men in violent crime, the figures show that, contrary to lazy folklore, fewer than 1% of them are involved in serious violence. Plenty of them are concentrating on doing well at school, even though there can be some sturdy obstacles to their progress in that sphere as well.

We read in Chapter 6 of Bernard Coard's proposition that the education system of the early 1970s rendered the West Indian child 'subnormal'. In particular, he was exercised by the idea that without forceful intervention, educational failure would result in the Black Caribbean community undergoing repeated cycles of economic and social deprivation. At the heart of his concern was the 'special' schools to into which so many Black children were dragooned: he might possibly recognise the ghost of these institutions in the Pupil Referral Units which, although light years away in terms of the provision on offer, still accommodate disproportionate numbers of Black pupils.

Numbers relating to the exclusion of pupils from schools in 2018-19, published by the Department for Education in July 2020, are alarming. Leaving aside children from Gypsy and Roma heritage, the figures for whom are a massive outlier, when it comes to being excluded from school, either temporarily or permanently, no other category comes remotely close to that of Black boys. One Black boy in ten underwent a period of temporary exclusion. One in 400 was permanently expelled. If you're looking for a sliver of 'good' news, it's that exclusion rates in all other ethnic groups worsened and that of Black boys marginally improved – but that remains a grim, statistical condemnation of a system that remains institutionally racist.

It is worth a brief digression to consider this most incendiary of expressions. It established itself in public discourse in 1999 with the publication of Sir William Macpherson's report into how the Metropolitan Police had dealt with the racist murder of a teenager, Stephen Lawrence, in south London in 1993. This was by no means the first use of the term, but the high-profile nature of the crime, and the bungled attempts to solve it, meant that it became widely recognised. The inquiry into the crime had started inauspiciously with the Met's immediate assumption that Lawrence and his friend, Duwayne Brooks, had clearly been up to no good. This, and a range of other inbuilt prejudices, hampered the efforts of the force and led Macpherson to the conclusion that 'a combination of professional incompetence, institutional racism and a failure of leadership' were the cause of this 'shambolic and shameful episode.'

The term was, and remains, widely misunderstood. For many people, especially those (like me) in public service, it seemed like a shocking affront. Did this accusation mean that we were racists? That could not possibly be the case, could it? To persist, just for a moment, with a personal perspective, it was left to a friend – a Black Brummie as it happens – to read the writing on the wall for me. I was grateful at the time and have been since, because I have often used the anecdote, complete with his scattergun expletives, to explain it to others. A bowdlerised version follows. Put baldly, he explained, it's not about you and your principles and actions – as worthy as they may be – it is about how institutions conduct themselves which then results in outcomes that consistently show that Black people have been disadvantaged. Macpherson, possibly more eloquently, but no more effectively, explained it as 'processes, attitudes and behaviour which amount to discrimination through unwitting prejudice, ignorance, thoughtlessness and racist stereotyping which disadvantages minority ethnic people'. It still plays out in multifarious ways, thirty years after Stephen Lawrence's murder by a gang of white racists and nearly sixty since the peremptory execution of a bewildered 20-year-old Jamaican.

Schools are not exempt. Apart from Black children being removed from mainstream schools in disproportionate numbers, Coard's other objection was that the curriculum on offer in English schools was narrow and culturally specific, thereby disadvantaging children from immigrant families. In the days before I started drafting this section, a startling illustration of what he meant presented itself.

In January 2021, the examination board Edexcel, faced with adjustments needed to its syllabus in the face of the Covid pandemic, decided to truncate the list of composers to be studied for Music A level. The section on modern music and jazz comprised The Beatles, Kate Bush and Courtney Pine: it was the latter, Black and British born, whom they decided to remove. It was a decision that was rescinded with some haste and with decent apology once its clumsiness had been pointed out. However, at a time when arguments about Black Lives Matter, footballers taking the knee and the proliferation of online racist abuse were regularly surfacing, quite why it didn't raise an immediate alarm in the offices of a body charged with examining the nation's children is, to say the least, disquieting. Were the antennae of those making the decision so insensitive that they failed to pick up any warning bleeps? Was their intention racist? Almost certainly not. Was the outcome of their action prejudicial? It's a question that barely requires a response.

Coard might also look at the current educational outcomes for Black children in the UK's schools with a degree of dismay. There has been some progress. In 1995 only 9% of Black A level students attained a place at a high-ranking university; by 2017 that had risen to 18%. Across, the piece, however, the examination results of Black students remain stubbornly low, despite some gradual, relative improvement over the last ten years. The way such judgements for 16-year-olds are made via

GCSE examinations requires some explanation and scrutiny.

A system dubbed Attainment 8 is in play, whereby there is a hierarchy of subjects, each bearing a specific tariff value, and an average sum of a child's worth is then calculated. Leaving aside the bluntness of this crude instrument, the subjects themselves tell a story: there has been almost no change from those at the centre of the school curriculum for some 75 years. There have been adjustments to content and emphases, but the bald truth is that it is a menu that offers much the same fayre as it has done for decades. If it reflects a set of values, it is those of the old, white, male, pale and stale. Many Black children do not prosper in such a framework.

In 2019, with Gypsy and Roma children again proving a startling exception, it was Black children of Caribbean heritage who lingered at the bottom of the Attainment 8 results table with a score of 39.4%. Just above them, with a score of 41%, are Black children of mixed heritage. These dismal figures, along with those relating to school exclusions, prejudicial treatment at the hands of the police, the greater likelihood of being a victim of crime and of receiving custodial sentences, paint a wretched picture. Speaking in 2019, Matthew Ryder, a QC who had been London's deputy mayor for integration, confidently asserted that for all its shortcomings, Macpherson had effected a sea-change in British society which was 'so significant (that) we have almost forgotten what it was like before'. There is little doubt that societal attitudes to race and racism are, indeed, unrecognisable from the world of Birmingham in the 1960s: it's just that for many Black youngsters this analysis is scant consolation for what they still have to endure.

In early 2021, I spoke to three Birmingham residents, all of Jamaican heritage and all of whom have made a significant mark on the society in which they now live and work. Beverley Lindsay holds honorary doctorates from two of Birmingham's universities, has been awarded the OBE and, in 2020, completed her term as Vice Lord-Lieutenant of the West Midlands – the first woman to hold the post. 'Not bad,' she tells me, without a hint of boastfulness, 'for a little girl who arrived from Jamaica' and was shocked to catch sight of the smoky, bedraggled lodging house that would become her first home in the city. 'I wondered why the car stopped where it did,' she grins. 'I thought we'd arrived at some sort of factory.' She tells me of how she and her family used to take Sunday walks after church to admire the manicured gardens and fine houses in Handsworth Wood. She hasn't strayed far from these first roots and is now – and I use the cliché unashamedly – a pillar of her community. Like many who came from her beloved homeland, she has worked unrelentingly to be successful; in her own case, she has overcome stacked odds and personal tragedy. She is a woman of enduring religious faith, is smilingly cheerful and great company. It is only when we begin to speak of the pall cast over parts of her community by drugs and violent crime that this positive disposition becomes a little frayed. She arrived in England after the death of Oswald Grey and when I tell her the story, she expresses despair and disappointment at this piece of history which chimes so clearly in modern times.

A couple of days later, I talk to Charlie Williams. He has been a tireless fighter in a range of anti-racist causes. 'I've honestly lost count of the number of protest marches and rallies I've organised,' he tells me. A quick search for him takes only seconds to verify his prominence, with numerous photographs of him cutting a dashing figure addressing street meetings, alongside some of his thoughtful comments and commentary. He is particularly enraged by the number of deaths of Black people in custody and even as he assures me that his figures are correct – and much as I have no reason to disbelieve him – I make a note to double-check their accuracy before committing them to print.

The bald truth, verified by sources ranging from the police

themselves, the Institute of Race Relations and the authoritative *Reality Check* team of the BBC, is that Black people are more than twice as likely to die while in police custody than their white counterparts. Just as shocking is the fact, verifiable from an even wider range of sources, that although there have been cases of police officers prosecuted for manslaughter, homicide or assault related to deaths in custody, none of these has been successful. The last time such a case resulted in a conviction was 1969 – closer to the era of Oswald Grey than that of George Floyd, whose public execution at the hands of a Minneapolis policeman made an impact on millions.

In our conversation about death in custody, I mention a current episode, the facts of which turn out to be familiar to Charlie. A fleeting, misread glimpse at a headline on a news website had led me to believe, momentarily, that there had been some developments in Cardiff about the case of Mahmood Hussein Mattan, whose story was told in Chapter 2. A demonstration had been held outside a police station and, without looking closely, I assumed it was more activity from Black Lives Matter advocates maintaining a campaign about his mistreatment. I was wrong: in my haste, I had misread a name. On 8 January, Mahmoud Mohammed Hassan had been arrested in Cardiff following an alleged disturbance. He was released without charge the next morning but died later that day, leading to the demonstration which, in its turn, led to fines being issued to some taking part for infringing Covid lockdown regulations.

South Wales Police immediately reported itself to the Independent Office for Police Conduct (IOPC), in relation to Hassan's unexpected death. Its director, Catrin Evans, issued a statement to 'reassure people that we will carry out a thorough and independent investigation into the contact police had with Mr Hassan'. The solicitor for Hassan's family, Hilary Brown, was somewhat less bland. 'We want somebody to try to explain to us,' she asserted, 'why a young, healthy man was arrested by

South Wales Police with no apparent injuries to his body and as a result of being released from Cardiff Bay police station was badly marked with bruising and cuts, and within hours was dead.' As this book goes to print, no report is yet forthcoming, although there were initial suggestions that Hassan had come into contact with over 50 police officers during his overnight detention. Within days, 30,000 people had signed a petition demanding that the IOPC release CCTV footage that could reveal crucial evidence.

What to make of such an incident? To take solace from the fact that community action left the police with no choice other than to instigate a formal investigation into its own conduct? To allow ourselves to believe that established procedures would have left it with no option to do so even without public outcry? To applaud the fact that tens of thousands of people were prepared to organise a demand for justice? Or to acknowledge the grim fact that a young Black man of the same heritage as one who was wrongly hanged in the same city some seventy years ago, still finds himself in mortal danger when he comes up against the forces supposedly charged with the fair enforcement of law and order?

Charlie and I reflect for a moment on the grim irony that although a young Black man in Birmingham may not risk a state-sponsored death, carried out with chilling rituals that echo from past centuries, he may yet be fatally endangered when encountering premises built for his ostensible protection. Nowhere is this exemplified more acutely than in the instance of Birmingham man, Kingsley Burrell, who died in police custody in 2011 and whose case has not been allowed to lie, thanks to the efforts of his family and campaigners like Williams.

On 27 March 2011, 29-year-old Burrell, a father of three who suffered from psychotic episodes, phoned the police from a supermarket in Winson Green to tell them he believed that he and his five-year-old son were being threatened by a gunman. In a scene redolent of incalculable similar incidents, including the death of Stephen Lawrence, the immediate assumption of police arriving at the scene was that Burrell was a danger to others, somehow culpable and worthy of suspicion. He was detained by police, taken to the Mary Seacole Unit in Winson Green and from there to the Queen Elizabeth Hospital, where he died, still handcuffed, of a cardiac arrest. Three years later, a 100-page report from the Independent Police Complaints Commission, containing 846 observations, concluded that there were judicial cases at differing levels of severity to be answered by the three police officers at the centre of the episode.

An inquest jury ruled in 2015 that prolonged restraint had been a factor in Kingsley Burrell's death and that there had been a failure to provide basic medical attention. Alarmingly, in 2017, jurors at Birmingham Crown Court cleared all three policemen of perverting the course of justice. A year later, however, one of the trio, Paul Adey, was dismissed when an internal inquiry 'found him to be in breach of standards of professional behaviours, honesty and integrity'. His colleagues, Mark Fannon and Paul Greenfield, escaped punishment. What came to light during the investigation was a private Facebook group aimed at police officers with well over a thousand members calling for support for Adey. Charlie Williams, described in the *Birmingham Mail* as 'an ever present at demonstrations in support of Burrell' – an epithet he wears as a badge of honour – expressed little surprise at the existence of the social media group, about which rumours were rife. Nevertheless, he suggested, 'to actually see it there is significant and mind-blowing.'

Mistrust of the police among huge swathes of Birmingham's Black communities is endemic. To worsen an already fragile situation, Williams talks to me – half-smiling but mainly in anger – about a recent incident in Ladywood, a mile or so to the north of Lee Bank Road. In October 2020, two police officers left their car to investigate suspicious behaviour. On their return, they discovered that a notebook containing highly sensitive information about gang-related behaviour was missing. Lest anyone be taken in by the notion that this was a Keystone Cops moment, local clergyman and activist, Bishop Desmond Jaddo revealed that he had been approached by parishioners who had been told to 'make funeral arrangements' as a result of information arising from the theft. Charlie Williams is convinced that the incident is linked to yet another tragic event.

Less than a mile from Winson Green Prison in Linwood Road, Handsworth. On a dull, grey Thursday afternoon in the middle of a lockdown that clouded all who breathed its air with a deadening, stifling boredom, Keon Lincoln, a 15-year-old Black boy, was set upon by a gang of kids near his house and was shot and stabbed before he died there. There was an agonizing inevitability to all that followed. His grieving mother talked of the 'infectious laugh that lit up the room whenever he was in it' and of a boy who was 'fun-loving and full of life'. The policeman leading the investigation acknowledged the shock to the whole community and condemned the 'inconceivable level of violence in broad daylight on a residential street'. On the possibility of the murder being gang-related, a local pastor, Neville Popo, proclaimed that 'the postcode war needs to stop: we now have to learn to respect each other and love each other in the way that we ought to love each other.' It could all have been a shabbily scripted, second-rate drama – except that it was very much for real and had been played out on a Birmingham street at the end of what should have been a normal school day.

In the days that follow the murder, I speak again to Bishop Joe Aldred. Even though he's recently retired and basking in the glow of relinquished responsibilities, his hackles rise when our conversation drifts towards this catastrophe, streets away from his former ministry. Yes, he concedes, there have been vigils and an outpouring of grief, but just days later the event is already fading from the headlines and, apart from Keon's nearest and dearest, it will soon have evaporated into the ether. 'Somehow,' rails Joe, 'we're not as outraged by a Black boy killed by other Black boys in Handsworth as we are by a whole array of other crimes.' It's impossible to disagree; impossible, too, not to imagine a metaphorically resigned, if sorrowful, shrug of the shoulders in the media reportage of the event.

A Black boy killed in Birmingham and it soon fades from our memory. As with every Brummie of a certain age I've ever spoken to, the miserable tale of Oswald Grey was unknown to Bishop Joe – although, to be fair, he only arrived from Jamaica in 1968. We're only able to guess at what went on in most of Grey's short life and most of what we are able to glean paints a dispiriting picture. He does not appear to have been the victim of an egregious miscarriage of justice and his was not the glamourous life of the high-rolling, loveable rascal. Bewildered and confused, short of money and prospects, living in a dingy bedsit, he must have known one thing with iron certainty: this England, this Birmingham, was most definitely not the promised land. If he was the person, and it looks entirely plausible that it was, who sidled into Thomas Bates's shop on that evening in June 1962 shakily pointing the stolen pistol which inflicted such misery on the shopkeeper's family, he was guilty of a shambolic, botched attempt to put a few quid into his empty pockets. It was no rollicking heist: he was not robbing the Deadwood stagecoach to stick it to the soulless, faceless company. He was no people's champion and this book does not attempt to paint him as such. But he was, most definitely, a victim of a whole set of forces, some of which remain horribly familiar and still cramp and constrain the lives of so many who live on Lee Bank and its surrounding streets.

The brief history of Oswald Grey has, I hope, been worth the telling. I have tried to recapture something of the world that he found in Birmingham as well as the world that moved on after his death. I have tried to place him in the habits, beliefs and social expectations of his times – and have looked for echoes in a world which, in 2021, is unrecognisable from its predecessor, never mind that of six decades ago. This has not been an attempt to rescue a hero, merely to save the memory of a boy who trod the same streets as me, probably caught the same buses as me, and who, at least, deserves a nod towards his unhappy existence and everything that it prompts us to reflect upon.

Oswald Augustus Grey. 1942-1962. Your life matters.

Postscript after a year of lockdown. How Covid was allowed to discriminate and why our rulers remained deafto systemic racism.

Most of this book was written at the height of the Covid-19 pandemic and it would be strange if it had ignored this shattering upheaval. During this time, a shocking statistical pattern arose. It emerged that people of colour were much more likely to contract the disease than white people and, once infected, much more likely to be admitted to intensive care and to die from its effects.

In October 2020, the Office for National Statistics (ONS) released the third of its reports into ethnic contrasts in deaths involving the virus. A trend that had been identified in its two earlier pieces of research became more firmly validated as the disease ran its course. The document begins with stark findings. 'Males and females of Black and South Asian ethnic background,' it revealed, 'were shown to have increased risks of death ... compared with those of White ethnic background'. In more specific terms, it informs us that 'males of Black African ethnic background had the highest rate of death (of) 2.7 times higher than males of White ethnic background; females of Black Caribbean ethnic background had the highest rate, 2.0 times higher than females of White ethnic background'. Such figures really do speak for themselves.

In early March 2021, the actor David Harewood, born and bred in Small Heath – a couple of miles east of Lee Bank Road – noted this data with alarm. He decided to make a BBC documentary entitled with blunt simplicity, *Why is Covid Killing More People of Colour?* It makes for compelling, if dispiriting viewing. He spends some time revisiting his native city where he chats with his sister about how the persistence of the casual racism that had been stitched into their childhood, even if it now does so a touch more discreetly. His sister demonstrates the forced smile of the job interviewer who clearly had not envisaged black skin when phoning to ask her to attend. For everyone to whom he speaks – with the one startling exception to come – racism is definitely not an issue that has been consigned to history.

The medical opinion, scientific research and reliable data about Covid combine to paint a picture of startling clarity. It hits Black people harder than white. No shred of credible evidence exists to suggest any possibility of these disparities being attributable to genetic features. What is clear, however, is that a range of societal indicators, such as how and where people live, how and where they work, how they are treated once there, as well as disturbingly stubborn ingrained racism – albeit some of it unconscious – all contribute to indisputable outcomes of health inequality.

Poor housing, lack of exercise and careless, unhealthy diets are congruent with two of the principal comorbidities which make serious illness with Covid more likely – diabetes and obesity. These are the disadvantages of those already disadvantaged – the poor. Asthma and other respiratory conditions which exacerbate the effects of Covid are more prevalent in those who live and work close to busy roads. Those who live in multi-generational households and those who have no option other than to go out to work, even when they believe that they are endangering themselves and their family by doing so, are the most susceptible to the worst effects of the virus. All these categories of enhanced vulnerability correspond with shocking certainty to the experience of Black people.

In London, 34% of those working in the most exposed occupations of health, food production and public transport come from Black and minority ethnic backgrounds. In the early months of the first lockdown in Spring 2020, an estimated 500 healthcare workers – low paid, non-unionised, largely Black – died from the disease. In terms of housing, Black people are

110% more likely to live in deprived neighbourhoods than their white counterparts – a figure that rises to an astonishing 114% for people with Bangladeshi heritage and an eye-watering 246% for those from Pakistani backgrounds. Beyond this, a Black man is three times more likely to suffer from hypertension, dementia, stroke and cancer than a white male. When it comes to mental health, he is ten times more likely to suffer from a serious psychological condition and is four times more likely to be sectioned under mental health legislation. This miserable tale does not end here.

The longitudinal research of Dr Jenny Douglas and others at The Open University has demonstrated that Black women are five times more likely to die in childbirth and its aftermath than white mothers. If that were not scandalous enough, her work has exposed the common experience of the hundreds of Black expectant mothers which revealed a disturbingly common feature. 'They're not listened to,' she tells David Harewood. 'Time and again, Black women told me that they were seen by health professionals as over aggressive and demanding,' she reveals, before going on to talk of the worrying finding that some medical practitioners believed that Black women were capable of withstanding greater degrees of pain than others. This raw, racist stereotype is also widely reported by Black men in their interactions with the health service. Harewood talks of the corrosive, debilitating effect of such discrimination in the lives of Black people in their dealings with everything from school, to work, to the police and to the health service. He uses the terms 'systematic' and 'structural', as opposed to 'institutional', and is in no doubt that it is at play when it comes to explaining the disproportionate numbers of Black Covid deaths. He uses his public profile to take his concerns to where it should count.

As his film draws to a close we see a shot of him watching Equalities Minister, Kemi Badenoch, offering an explanation to the House of Commons for these worrying inequalities of health outcomes. She does not shy away from statistics and figures that are incontrovertible. The House – such as it is with most members operating remotely – is asked to note the seriousness of the issue and to be reassured that her office will consider how best to redress matters. Harewood seems sceptical but is pleased to have set up a video call with the minister in an attempt to delve a little deeper into her analysis and prospective actions.

It turns out to be an extraordinary – and illuminating – episode. Badenoch readily concedes that the fundamental reasons for disproportionate numbers of Black deaths relate to underlying health conditions, occupation and general living standards. Just look around my workplace, she explains, and notice how the catering, security and cleaning staff are largely people of colour. She understands. She gets it. Harewood, a trained actor by profession, remains calmly insistent. Why is this the case, he wants to know. Why are so many Black people in such precarious situations, both at home and at work? Oh, it's not the case everywhere here at Westminster, she retorts. Look at me. Look at the Chancellor. Things are on the up – and education will be the key. Harewood gives it one last shot: she does know that education is not immune to structural racism … and … while we're at it, why, Minister, in your explanation about these disparities in health outcomes, have you never once mentioned the R word?

Badenoch studied for her law degree at Birkbeck, University of London. It's an institution founded on radical thinking. When Dr George Birkbeck opened its doors to the 'mechanics', the working men of London, in 1823, he proclaimed that 'now is the time for the universal blessings of the benefits of knowledge'. By 1830, he'd taken the unprecedented step of allowing women to study there. It remains a shining testament to enlightened, progressive educational approaches. It is almost impossible to believe that an alumna of such an organisation from the early twenty-first century would need to have the concept of systemic racism explained to her. Yet with the firm resolve of either the zealot or the dull simpleton, the Minister for Equalities offers a dead bat to any questions about such an explanation. The boy from Small Heath declares himself 'frustrated'; his restraint is to be admired.

By the time the virus had taken firm hold in April 2020, it was becoming clear to physicians that Black people were at greater risks from its effects than other ethnic groups. At Birmingham's Queen Elizabeth Hospital, it was recorded that 64% of deaths were of people of colour. Consultant nephrologist, Dr Anan Sharif expressed a 'personal hunch ... that it's more social factors and that kind of data doesn't really exist in hospitals.' His experience on the ground was a further reflection of the findings in an article in the *British Medical Journal* (BMJ) which had expressed 'concerns about a possible association between ethnicity and outcome ... after the first 10 doctors in the UK to die from covid-19 were identified as being from ethnic minorities'. By December, a further BMJ article, authored by a number of Birmingham-based physicians, reported on their data that 'those of South Asian ethnicity appear at risk of worse COVID-19 outcomes'. While suggesting that social factors played an equal part with comorbidities, they concluded by suggesting that 'further studies need to establish the underlying mechanistic pathways'.

Underlying mechanistic pathways, indeed. It might just be that those pathways, built on layers of suspicion, prejudice and ignorance, can be tracked right back to a society which was complicit in, and then forgetful of, the summary disposal of a bemused young immigrant from Jamaica on a gloomy day in Birmingham in November 1962.

As the countries of the United Kingdom planned their tentative steps out of lockdown in the early Spring of 2021, a report was published which might have been greeted with quiet satisfaction by Badenoch and her political bedfellows, even though most of them maintained a diplomatic – and possibly embarrassed – silence about it. The Sewell Commission produced its findings on the Racial and Ethnic Disparities in the UK and drew the confident conclusion that 'the roots of advantage and disadvantage for different groups are complex, and often as much to do with social class, 'family' culture and geography as ethnicity'. Its author, Tony Sewell, is British-born to Jamaican parents and his career is shining testament to the rewards to be gained from hard work, determination and a refusal to be cowed by stacked odds. In recent years, he has revelled in the role of outspoken contrarian and has been particularly withering about what he characterises as cultures of weak-minded excuse-making by sections of Black communities. Unsurprisingly, he is cast by supporters and detractors as both hero and villain, poster-boy and sell-out merchant. Nonetheless, he must have been disappointed by the tepid reception afforded his labours from those from whom he might have expected more.

Perhaps it was the almost concurrent resignation of Samuel Kasumu, one of the government's principal advisers on race that accounted for this muted response. There was the damnation of faint praise encompassed in the Prime Minister's observation that it was 'an interesting piece of work' but that he wouldn't 'say the Government is going to agree with absolutely everything in it.' He went on to acknowledge, with his characteristic breeziness when attending to detail, that it had 'some original and stimulating work in it that I think people need to read and to consider.' In other words, of course he was indicating that he hadn't actually read it but, significantly, even he was not prepared to publicly espouse Sewell's analysis that disadvantage and discrimination could be explained by fecklessness and a lack of ambition.

If Sewell had been hoping for something more encouraging from Britain's main online Black newspaper, *The Voice*, for whom he had once been a regular correspondent, he would have been similarly disappointed. Under a headline declaring that 'A commission led by people that deny the reality and existence of institutional racism was always going to be a whitewash' the paper lists a collection of quotations from a range of activists expressing dismay at the report's contents. This disappointment was reflected in an exasperated chorus from a broad swathe of organisations, encompassing education unions, religious organisations, equality trusts and academics. Despite Sewell's protestation to the *Daily Telegraph* podcast that he was 'fairly thick-skinned' and 'used to' such reactions, it's difficult to imagine that he was doing anything other than donning the bravest of faces.

In his consideration of Covid, Sewell showed himself afflicted by the same blind spot when it came to connecting class and race as Badenoch had done in her conversation with David Harewood. The report concedes that Black and Asian people are more vulnerable because of increased risk of exposure, going on to observe that 'this is attributed to the fact that Black and South Asian people are more likely to live in urban areas with higher population density and levels of deprivation' and to 'work in higher risk occupations such as healthcare and transport, and to live with older relatives who themselves are at higher risk'. It is the stubborn notion that there is no relationship between where people live and work and their race that Sewell's critics found so frustrating. The writer Anatole France's famous observation from the nineteenth century that 'the law, in its majestic equality, forbids the rich as well as the poor to sleep under bridges, to beg in the streets and to steal bread' seems to have informed the thinking of the learned Dr Sewell and the equally obtuse Equalities Minister.

His report, notwithstanding his intentions to the contrary, served to emphasise the centrality of race as a determinant of health and prosperity. The first year of a pandemic that destabilised society in a way that was previously unimaginable, demonstrated that many of the ideas and attitudes that accounted for the demise of Oswald Augustus Grey decades earlier were not ready to be consigned to oblivion. Covid-19 laid bare divisions in British society that became glaringly unavoidable: don't be poor, don't live in shabby housing, don't be Black – whether it's 1962 or 2021.

Most ethnic minority groups have a higher risk of death involving COVID-19 than those of White British background

- Patterns of coronavirus (COVID-19) mortality risk by ethnic group changed over the course of the pandemic.
- In the first wave of the pandemic (24 January to 11 September 2020), people of Black and South Asian ethnic background had a substantially higher risk of death involving COVID-19, compared with those of White British background.
- In the second wave of the pandemic (12 September 2020 onwards), people of Bangladeshi and Pakistani ethnic background were particularly at risk; while people of Black ethnic background remained at higher risk in the second wave, the relative risk compared with White British people was reduced.

The Office of National Statistics. 21 September 2021

Acknowledgements

For the most part, I have identified in the text those people whose work I have raided, those whose testimony I have relied upon and those whose brains I have picked. There are others whose research, scholarship and advice have not been named and so I express my gratitude to Colin Brock, Carl Chinn, Kieran Connell, Oliver Durose, Rosemary Cragg, Ian Francis, Amelia Gentleman, Alice Gradwell, Gavin Hales, Jean Hill, Jim Hill, Matthew Hilton, Roger King, David Kopel, Chris Lewis, James McKay, Seamus Milne, Richard Norton-Taylor, Joseph Olsen, Lyttanya Shannon, Daniel Silverstone, Donald Thomas, Talia Tobias, Satnam Virdee, Andrew Walmington and Jonathan Watkins. If, somehow, I've left you out, well … in a piece of work that laments the airbrushing from history of an event of significance, I'm trusting that you'll appreciate the irony while accepting my apologies.

Sources

The text often makes the sources of information clear. This is a book written in the digital age and I have adopted the view that inquisitive readers whose imagination and interest has been piqued by mention of a person, an event, a film or a report, will be able to follow their noses, beginning with a simple click and then following the trail with however much energy and persistence they believe it merits. That's certainly what I did. I reiterate my comment in the preface: there is plenty of opinion here, but all facts, quotations and statistics gleaned from published material can be easily located.

As I have been at pains to point out throughout, finding any living person with a reliable recollection of this event has been almost impossible. The closest I have come is a few rather unreliable or hazy contributions on social media platforms. As

I point out in Chapter 5, the closely-guarded court papers may have revealed information that could have told us more about Felix and Oswald Grey in particular, but the National Archive and the Information Commissioner insist that such material should be more closely guarded than the deliberations of Her Majesty's Cabinet. If any readers know more than I have been able to locate here, I would be delighted to hear from them at j.berry@herts.ac.uk.

About the author

Jon Berry is a retired teacher and now part-time university lecturer. He has written widely about education and, in recent years, football. He writes a regular blog on politics and current affairs. Although no longer living in Birmingham, he is a proud Brummie, still clinging to hope over experience with his Birmingham City season ticket.

By the same author
Project Restart. From the Prem to the parks, how
football came out of lockdown.

Hugging Strangers. The frequent lows and occasional
highs of football fandom.

Boomeranting.
Putting the test in its place. How to teach well and
keep the number-crunchers quiet.

Teachers Undefeated.

Teachers' legal rights and responsibilities.

CHRONOS
BOOKS

HISTORY

Chronos Books is an historical non-fiction imprint. Chronos publishes real history for real people; bringing to life people, places and events in an imaginative, easy-to-digest and accessible way - histories that pass on their stories to a generation of new readers.
If you have enjoyed this book, why not tell other readers by posting a review on your preferred book site.

Recent bestsellers from Chronos Books are:

Lady Katherine Knollys
The Unacknowledged Daughter of King Henry VIII
Sarah-Beth Watkins
A comprehensive account of Katherine Knollys' questionable
paternity, her previously unexplored life in the Tudor court
and her intriguing relationship with Elizabeth I.
Paperback: 978-1-78279-585-8 ebook: 978-1-78279-584-1

Cromwell was Framed
Ireland 1649
Tom Reilly
Revealed: The definitive research that proves the Irish nation
owes Oliver Cromwell a huge posthumous apology for
wrongly convicting him of civilian atrocities in 1649.
Paperback: 978-1-78279-516-2 ebook: 978-1-78279-515-5

Why The CIA Killed JFK and Malcolm X
The Secret Drug Trade in Laos
John Koerner
A new groundbreaking work presenting evidence that the CIA
silenced JFK to protect its secret drug trade in Laos.
Paperback: 978-1-78279-701-2 ebook: 978-1-78279-700-5

The Disappearing Ninth Legion
A Popular History
Mark Olly
The Disappearing Ninth Legion examines hard evidence for the
foundation, development, mysterious disappearance, or possi-
ble continuation of Rome's lost Legion.
Paperback: 978-1-84694-559-5 ebook: 978-1-84694-931-9

Beaten But Not Defeated
Siegfried Moos - A German anti-Nazi who settled in Britain
Merilyn Moos
Siegi Moos, an anti-Nazi and active member of the German
Communist Party, escaped Germany in 1933 and, exiled in
Britain, sought another route to the transformation
of capitalism.
Paperback: 978-1-78279-677-0 ebook: 978-1-78279-676-3

A Schoolboy's Wartime Letters
An evacuee's life in WWII — A Personal Memoir
Geoffrey Iley
A boy writes home during WWII, revealing his own fascinating
story, full of zest for life, information and humour.
Paperback: 978-1-78279-504-9 ebook: 978-1-78279-503-2

The Life & Times of the Real Robyn Hoode
Mark Olly
A journey of discovery. The chronicles of the genuine historical
character, Robyn Hoode, and how he became one of England's
greatest legends.
Paperback: 978-1-78535-059-7 ebook: 978-1-78535-060-3